We Need To Talk

*Your Guide to Challenging
Business Conversations*

ANDREA J. LEE

We Need To Talk: Your Guide To Challenging Business Conversations

Published by Thought Partners International

Book cover and interior design by Delaine Ulmer,
StudioUltimateDesign.com

ISBN: 978-0-9862984-0-0

Printed in the United States of America.

Requests for permission to make copies of any part of this book can be
made to:
Thought Partners International
250-898-8786
support@wealthythoughtleader.com

TO MIKE

CONTENTS

Foreword

Life is precious. Humans are born and we live inside of relationships.

We either take responsibility for the state of our connections or we allow others to take control. Often it is a balance between the two.

This is the story for each and every one of us.

Some of us touch a few lives, others touch hundreds or even thousands and there are those few who touch millions.

While it is obvious that I cannot ever count how many people Andrea J. Lee has touched, I am sure that it is not hundreds or thousands. I am certain that it is close to the million mark.

Andrea's journey begins in Canada, to newly immigrated parents. She lived as a good and obedient child within the home and a good and rule following citizen outside the home.

Somewhere along the way, Andrea realized that the way to her own dreams and happiness was to go against the grain that many of her peers took. She started a business quite early in life, then she was the right hand of Thomas Leonard, the father of coaching.

Her journey with Leonard set her on the career path that she travels still today. His untimely death made a deep impression on her and she has strived to do as much as she can, for as many people as she can reach.

This new work "We need to talk," is yet another step on the journey to reach even more people.

I was extremely fortunate to have met Andrea in 2005, first just on the telephone, then in person. Her unyielding support for my dreams allowed me to continue to dream. The dream was highly unlikely to come true, but she held the faith even as I wavered and doubted.

This new work that Andrea has written is the culmination of many years of actually living and speaking the principles exposed here. From Truth Telling to Apologizing and Saying Graceful Goodbyes, she gives us simple and useful insight as to how to do these too often difficult things.

She has been teaching and honing her knowledge for many years and now she gives this knowledge to us.

It is very important to know that the content of We Need To Talk, must be practiced and used. It must be honed over time and in many situations. We must breathe in this book and then breathe it out into the world in ways that honor our selves and our dreams.

I have been witness to the birthing of 'We Need to Talk' and I can tell you it has given Andrea tremendous joy to write this for you. She wants you to read it, really read it and use it.

Andrea chooses very carefully how she publishes and distributes her work. It is her fervent wish that every person who buys it really takes the time to use it. She does not want it to gather dust on your bookshelf or nightstand.

It has been my greatest joy to witness Andrea's journey to this juncture and I intend to be with her way into the future.

Enjoy and digest and let her know how it resonates with you.

Indrani Goradia
Founder, Indrani's Light Foundation
www.indranislight.org

Introduction

"We need to talk."

What is it about those four little words that strike fear into the heart of the bravest business person?

And yes, I include myself in that group.

I was the woman sitting in a client's office, heart pounding, stomach in knots, covered in a sheen of perspiration – simply because I had something meaningful to say.

I was also a witness as a long line of secretaries (as they were called back then) quavered and cowered – and then quit, without saying much – when their boss yelled at them, spit flying, year after year.

And I also went through a period when I used anger as a weapon myself, in my personal relationships. I was the person people tiptoed around, hoping not to detonate.

That probably gives you some insight into why this book is such an important treatise to me.

It's why I've raced to get it done at a time when many other projects and people beckon. If I may put it succinctly, look around, and I think you will agree: there is some serious shit hitting the fan, people.

Sometimes the symptoms of un-had conversations don't make themselves this evident, and in a way, that's worse. We muddle along, thinking 'this is how it is' and live with the low-to-high-grade stress and adrenaline that run through the veins of too many entrepreneurs. But since these flare ups have happened, we may as well use them as a the signs they are – signs that something is not right, and if we could only talk more intelligently with each other…being in business for ourselves might not come with as high a cost.

I'm hitting my mid 40s this year. In what I'm reassured is a normal exercise for mid-life, I mentally scanned my 'resume' and realized I've been mentoring small and solo-businesses to achieve excellence for going on 15 years. Meanwhile, my own mentor, Thomas Leonard, who arguably founded the profession we know as coaching, and was a dyed-in-the-wool entrepreneur, died suddenly of a heart attack at the age of just 47. In this season of rapid change in both the bigger global picture, and in my own life, I asked myself, if I only had one project remaining to me, one final hurray that this brain, body and soul could muster, what must it be?

I determined it would be this.

"We Need to Talk" is the phrase that asked to be the title of this book. I want it to be at once very practical, as well as to give you a different way to look at your life as a player in the business world. I intend for there to be big and little-picture a-has, with real-life examples drawn from almost every adversarial circumstance a small business can go through. Don't worry though, the names have been changed so everyone can feel at ease while speculating about who, exactly, we might be talking about.

FOUR SMALL YET POWERFUL WORDS

When I came home from walking our dog Oz one day, my husband Mike said to me, "So you know the new book you're working on? It's called 'We Need to Talk' eh?"

Me, "Yep."

Mike: "Well, just so you know, and it might be fun to include in the book if it fits, the mock-up you made of the cover gave me a real start. I saw the sheet of paper with the title in big green capital letters and I thought you'd written me a note!"

With what Mike and I have been through together, we're proud of being able to laugh at that little incident. Becoming people who can peacefully navigate almost any conversation is definitely worth it.

In summary, as charged as this topic can be, I want to kick us off by saying, definitively:

Understanding what's happening when we're trying to talk to one another about difficult things, things we want very badly, or care about a lot, and looking at the point of these conversations…

…plus practicing having all manner of business conversations in a certain way, filled with life, alive with your desires, collaborating with the desires of others, and allowing you to create value in the world more precisely with less waste…

These are the goals of this book.

How do we get our great work done when so much is unsure and things are fraught with so many subtleties and nuances?

When it comes to leading a team, sharing money with partners, dealing with unhappy clients, putting a stop to ineffective meetings, or even saying we're sorry, how can we have these conversations well? How can we allow uncertainty to be present and lead well, while still not falling into absolutes, or having a my-way-or-the-highway mentality?

How do we get the strategic and granular things done as business people, consistently and easily, avoiding lapsing into silence or being corroded by anger?

What about practical ways to do certain things in business that are inherently sticky or tricky?

These are the answers I want you to have for the time you invest in reading. But that's me.

You tell me what happens for you, okay?

*"A smooth sea never
made a skillful sailor."*

ENGLISH PROVERB

CHAPTER 1

What I Wish
I Could Say

Being privy to so many of the inner trials and tribulations of business owners as their coach, I've had some time to accumulate observations, and I'd like to share one with you.

I believe the playing field we call business today is the single biggest battlefield of human relationships in existence. And it continues to grow.

With more people engaging in business relationships now than ever, this also makes business the biggest arena of suffering when it comes to difficult conversations. That honor used to go to marital discord, but most people just divorce these days and don't bother with talking.

Business owners, not so much. We tend to be stubborn about our vision for our work, and we walk around with the stress of pent-up conflict in our blind spot, like an illness we don't realize we have.

Let's take a pause and bring your specific circumstances into the conversation, shall we? Even in a book, I'd prefer for this to be a two-way meeting of the minds, so let me ask you a few questions:

On a scale of 1 to 10, with 10 being true, and 1 being untrue, how would you rank yourself on the following items? Feel free to circle directly on this page, or, answer in a notebook if you have a digital copy.

The Inner and Outer Conflict Assessment for People in Business

When I think of my clients, I have positive feelings about working with them.

UNTRUE									TRUE
1	2	3	4	5	6	7	8	9	10

I am confident that my plans for growth will bear fruit.

UNTRUE | | | | | | | | | TRUE
1 | 2 | 3 | 4 | 5 | 6 | 7 | 8 | 9 | 10

When I think of my team, including contractors, employees, vendors or suppliers, I have positive feelings about their contributions.

UNTRUE | | | | | | | | | TRUE
1 | 2 | 3 | 4 | 5 | 6 | 7 | 8 | 9 | 10

My family and friends do not tell me they're concerned about how much I work.

UNTRUE | | | | | | | | | TRUE
1 | 2 | 3 | 4 | 5 | 6 | 7 | 8 | 9 | 10

I have fear about meeting my financial obligations.

UNTRUE | | | | | | | | | TRUE
1 | 2 | 3 | 4 | 5 | 6 | 7 | 8 | 9 | 10

When I have a challenging situation to handle, I can calmly do what's needed.

UNTRUE | | | | | | | | | TRUE
1 | 2 | 3 | 4 | 5 | 6 | 7 | 8 | 9 | 10

I feel equipped to start and hold challenging business conversations of all kinds.

UNTRUE | | | | | | | | | TRUE
1 | 2 | 3 | 4 | 5 | 6 | 7 | 8 | 9 | 10

To submit your answers for inclusion in a confidential database, go to
www.wealthythoughtleader.com/conflictassessment

While being proficient at handling difficult business conversations isn't the complete answer to all of the above challenges, it's certainly a path to getting there. Because not handling those conversations will definitely lead to stress. If you scored 5 or less on 3 or more of the categories, you almost certainly carry an intense level of stress, and are most likely dealing with adrenaline in your body on a regular basis. This translates into fatigue, a loss of rationality, and lack of clarity – all of which handcuff you and prevent you from creating excellence.

If you scored 6 or more in 3 or more of the categories, you're likely functioning very well, and you have the opportunity to do even better if you decide to go the extra mile. The best businesses, the ones that fulfill the greater calling of their vision, are extra-milers in this way – just my opinion.

But whatever your scores are, they are yours to change. It doesn't have to take a lot of effort or time, just intention. It can be done! And together we can create a story in which' the rest the same.

As we learn to do our business conversations well, we'll understand how to do our other difficult conversations better too – with our families, our leaders, even ourselves. The more the better!

Whatever your motivation is for digging in, let's go further in each category to surface some of the nuances. It doesn't matter if you have a little or lot of pressure on you, these diagnostic questions can help identify the nature of the problem more clearly, starting with:

YOUR CLIENTS

We can't always have perfect clients all the time. But when we have upset clients, or we are upset with clients, not knowing what to say can make things worse very quickly, or, even worse, allow them to fester. It only takes one unhappy client situation, especially a major one, to take the stuffing out of an excellent plan for growth.

Do you have clients who push your boundaries, consistently asking for more than you agreed to provide? What about clients who stubbornly don't act on your advice and then complain about the results or lack thereof? Of course, there are the clients who don't pay on time, don't honour appointments, treat your team or you with disrespect. Sometimes, there are totally abusive, toxic clients that somehow find their way to us.

What other ways do clients create difficult conversations for you in your business? Try these specific questions on the folloowing pages to surface the specifics in your life:

Fill in the Blank:

1. In my wildest dreams, I would tell my client…

2. For this client, I wish I didn't have to…

3. If I could, and I knew how, I would fire this client because…

4. The negative emotions I feel when it comes to this client are…

5. I wish this client would…

That should be a good start to understanding what you're living with, and where you are now, when it comes to conversations you could be having with clients.

For each of the following sets of questions, answer as specifically as you can, and give yourself the autonomy to adapt the questions so they're perfect for you. You may use slightly different language – feel free to change it to suit you. Let's get to the bottom of where the most challenging, most draining, most expensive un-had conversations live in your world. Then, in Chapter Two, we'll get going with the solutions.

YOUR FINANCIAL PICTURE

Fill in the Blank:

1. If only my income was…

2. My fees and price points should be…

WE NEED TO TALK   Andrea J. Lee

3.   The amount of money going out in expenses is…

4.   In my ideal world, my debt…

5.   For me, I wish splitting up money with partners or collaborators was…

YOUR TEAM

[0 . If only I had a team I could…]

1. The things I wish my team would understand and change are...

2. When I consider what the team gets compensated, I feel...

3. I get embarrassed or angry because sometimes, my team...

4. Even after lots of attempts at communicating, my team still...

5.   When my back is turned, I'm afraid that my team…

6.   In my wildest dreams, my team would…

YOUR SELF

1.   My business is serving me and my life in some areas, but in other areas it…

2.   I wish my workload was…

3. My health and energy levels are…

4. If I could describe my inner self-talk - what I talk to myself about regarding my business - it would sound like…

5. I suspect that I have other unspoken, internal conflict about…

6. If I could wave a magic wand in my life and the role work and business plays in it, I would…

YOUR COMMUNICATION

1. My most recent challenging business conversation was about…

2. Of the un-had conversations I have accumulated, I can think of the following…

3. If I were able to have just 1 or 2 excellent conversations, they would be the following, and having them well would bring me…

4. When I think about having the most difficult conversations, I typically feel…

5. When it comes to my communication, I wish…

As the battlefield of un-had conversations inside you comes to light, consider pausing a moment to take stock. To the degree you've unearthed the truth, you might be experiencing a reality check. It's okay to be momentarily disheartened. The myth of business people as stubbornly idealistic and positive has been around a long time. There's nothing the matter with recognizing you'd like things to be different.

In fact, to make change, we need to be fearlessly candid about our reality, instead. As the field of entrepreneurship grows each year, our ability to have great conversations about the toughest of things is going to play a huge role in creating a world we love living in. We have the tools to do it, and some of them are in this book. Now we just need to use them.

COACH'S NOTE

I would prefer you take small, sure steps in the right direction, acknowledging reality, rather than hide from the problem and race ahead in the wrong direction, hoping something good might happen. Beware going full speed ahead, with confidence, in the wrong direction.

This goes for challenging business conversations and your business strategy as a whole.

For a complete set of questions in this chapter, go to

www.wealthythoughtleader.com/conflictassessment

where you can print a downloadable version for your own use, or, to explore going further with a coach as your partner, fill in the questions online and request a no-pressure, exploratory conversation.

"Do the best you can until you know better. Then, when you know better, do better."

MAYA ANGELOU

CHAPTER 2

The Universal Key

It's said that most books are never read, and that even if they are, it's rare to get past the first 30 pages. Well here we are, and you're still here, so I want to spill the beans while I have your attention.

If you don't read beyond this chapter, I'd at least like for you to have the universal key to detangling most of the most difficult conversations I've witnessed in 15+ years of business. This key is a little bit like the universal blood type

"O" which every blood type can receive in a transfusion. I call it the Delta Model.

As you likely know, "delta" is the fourth letter of the Greek alphabet, and the symbol for it is a triangle, used in science to represent change. The Delta Model provides us a simple thinking structure for conversations with a goal. If you're having a conversation in which you're trying to 'get somewhere,' or help someone else 'get somewhere,' this model will work. The thinking structure can be outlined thusly:

STEP #1:
Find out where your
conversation partner
is right now. (Point A.)

STEP #2:
Find out where your
conversation partner
wants to go. (Point B.)

STEP #3:
Together, come up with
suggestions for how you
can get from A to B.

What do I mean by conversation partner? It's worth pointing out that this could be any other human being, including a client, team member, vendor, partner, or even yourself, in your own head. We all talk to ourselves and try to get somewhere in those conversations, so we may as well do it well, right?

To go along with the thinking construct, there are three questions that make the Delta Model essentially foolproof to apply. You can embellish, or put the questions in your own words as you go, taking into account the nature of your relationships. But we can boil it all down to this: ***Where are you now? Where do you want to go? How do you want to get there?*** *(See Figure 1 on page 34.)*

To start unpacking this model, let's do a straightforward, non-business example to illustrate:

The setting is summer. Your conversation partner is a young child who is crying. Something is amiss and you'd like to help. You apply the steps:

Step #1: Where are you now?

"Why are you crying, little one?"

"I ate all the cherries and now there's no more cherries."

"Oh, that's sad."

"Yes."

Figure 1

The 3 Points of the Delta Model for Challenging Conversations

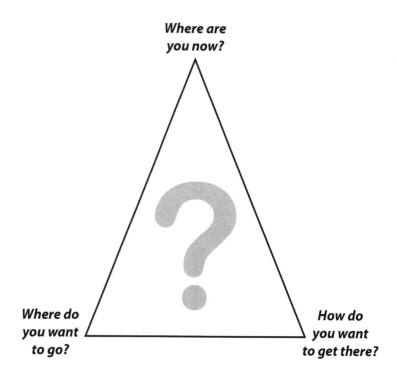

Where are you now?

Where do you want to go?

How do you want to get there?

Step #2: Where do you want to go?

"What would make it better, sweetie?"

"More cherries!"

Step #3: How do you want to get there?

"Okay well I have some cherries left, can I give you half, or try some apples?"

"Half!"

If only all business conversations could sound like this, right? The point is, even if the solution isn't as simple, the structure for the conversation can be, when using the Delta Model. The difference between point 1 and 2 is the delta -- the change that's desired. The more truthful the answers are to each question, the more robust the results, and that's where some skill and experience will help. We'll cover more of this in the next chapter, "You Can Handle the Truth."

Allowing the 3-step thinking structure to sink in, I suspect you will start to hear it in lots of places, even when it's not being done on purpose. We'll do more with the Delta Model throughout the book, especially in the sample templates and conversations, but for now, a few final comments on the universal-ness of this tool.

Useful one-on-one or in groups, making you look good in a pinch

The Delta questions are useful for nitty-gritty one-on-one conversations, as well as for bigger groups. They are excellent tools to pull out in a meeting that's run amok, particularly if you can find a way to say, "Whoa… this meeting seems to have run amok, could I suggest a way to structure our conversation with three questions?"

You can even whip out the three questions when you're put on the spot to lead any kind of conversation, and you'll see how well it serves you.

Removes hidden agendas, builds credibility and trust

If you've never experienced being the 'Switzerland' in a given conversation and think you might like it, there's one more reason to make the Delta Model one of your go-to's as a business person.

People readily rally under a structure that, in its simplicity, doesn't seem to have a hidden agenda. You might be surprised at how much more trustworthy you're perceived to be when you lead in this way.

Removes excess emotion

Heated debates and tough negotiations can also thrive under the 3-questions model, because excess emotion gets removed. You'll see more examples in the specific problem-solving chapters to come, but here is a taster:

Have the participants in the meeting answer the three questions, and based on their answers, you will quickly see if there is overlap. If there is, you can proceed to negotiate an agreement that meets at least some of the needs of everyone.

If there isn't any overlap, it will become clear to everyone that there isn't, and the parties can agree to stop trying to force an agreement, a victory in itself! Or, they may discover their willingness to re-state their answers to questions 1 and 2 and try again.

Gets to 'how' not just 'what' to make change stick

Finally, back to using the Delta questions on you. Don't let the third question fool you. It addresses what I believe are the deal breakers that are so often hidden, namely the manner in which you'd like to achieve your goal, not just what you want to achieve.

Let's say the scenario is you and you'd like to raise your fees. Or, you're a business advisor and you're helping your client with this:

Step 1: Where are you now?

"The business expenses keep going up, and I'm starting to feel resentful of all the work my team and I deliver for the price. I discovered that what I'm charging is on the low side compared to other people in my field."

Step 2: Where would you like to go?

"I'd like to raise them to at least 25% higher than they are now. That way, my profit margin would be reasonable and I could pay the team a bit more. I would feel more properly rewarded and be able to wow the client better, too."

Step 3: How do you want to get there?

"I want to do it professionally and not seem desperate. I think it's reasonable to raise my prices, but I also want to treat existing clients with respect. Maybe I'll give 45 days notice that the fees will be going up so they can be prepared, and invite clients who want to pre-purchase more work from us to do so within 45 days at half the increase."

How – in what manner – the delta, or change, is achieved, is as important as achieving the delta itself. If you were successful in raising your fees but, in the scenario above, lost the clients' respect, an important part of the goal would have been missed. For results you can be proud of, and especially if you have a history of reaching an agreement, only to have it fall apart later, give each of the three questions in the Delta Model their full due.

Cuts through complexity

The most complex conversations often have a great deal of jeopardy attached, for example, when a big consulting firm gets a call from their biggest client saying 'We're unhappy.' In cases like these, I suggest that you throw everything out and carefully offer the Delta questions. By putting just a few key things back on the table for the conversation, you can often sidestep the baggage and history that's gumming up the machinery.

> **PREDICTION:**
>
> Use the universal 3-step thinking structure and corresponding three questions well, and I, and many other business mentors, will soon have much less work to do. Bring it on!

Section I

Problem Solving

"Not to put a turd in the soup, but..."

LINDA BALLEW

CHAPTER 3

Telling the Truth Effectively

Of all the aspects of the topic of charged conversations, there is just one that qualifies as 'haunting' to me – how to tell the truth well, especially in the face of high emotion. Let's take these one at a time, and then together.

What is it that makes telling the truth so hard? So much of what untangles challenging situations is the ability to truth-tell, so what makes us so constipated about it? I've come to the conclusion that we actually want to tell the truth, but lose track of that desire. Several main things get in the way.

1. **First, we don't think we'll be heard.** The truth, like saffron, is precious and rare, measured by the single strand. Why speak it, if it's only going to be carried off by a passing breeze? This alone is a strong deterrent to speaking up. Why bother?

2. **Next, supposing we are heard, the reactions are unpredictable, and they can sometimes even be violent.** Truths, told directly, can be too intense, like undiluted apple juice concentrate. Something that at the right strength can be refreshing and enjoyable is, instead, spit-out-worthy. Too much! Not like that, thanks.

   Told in the usual way, straight on, after holding back and holding in for a long time, we should expect to have to step away from the truth quickly. It's like lighting the fuse of a truth-bomb.

3. **And third, we're unaccustomed to speaking plainly.** Where, in fact, would you say the truth gets told in your life or business, reliably? Not in newspapers – well, in good journalism, hopefully a certain kind of factual truth gets told. But there is a greater truth than just the facts, as well, that doesn't get addressed. How about in close relationships, such as with our parents? Regrettably, families are

often places where untruths are most in-grown, like candida in the belly, with its spikes that puncture the stomach wall and cause leaky gut.

No, the truth has historically been protected and private, occurring only occasionally, say once a week, if you're pious, in the confessional between priest and devotee. Between a king and his special advisor, consigliore, or banished friend. Consider Shakespeare, who wrote monologues for his heroes, the better for them to have a place to share the truth. If we're lucky, we too, tell the truth when we're by ourselves – just not in rhyming couplets, or sonnet-style.

There's something about the human condition that's revealed in our inconsistent relationship with truth, isn't there? Food for thought.

To advance your ability to have more honest conversations, let's take these obstacles to the truth one at a time and see whether we can get them to back off enough to create some space. What we want is lots of opportunity to practice truth-saying starting with low-risk situations, so you can become a natural, elegant teller of truths.

This ability to tell the truth effectively will most certainly set you apart as a business leader, and weaken even the gnarliest of your business challenges.

THE LANGUAGE OF TRUTH-TELLING

When it comes to the first two reasons we don't habitually speak the truth, we can approach them with a single change of framework. Truths need to be spoken in a certain way in order to be heard. If spoken in that way, taking into account the potential for excessive emotion, and with protective measures for our own well being, they become little miracles. The trick, of course, is to learn how to say them in this way.

CREATING THE INTERRUPT

This is an important first step. If the flow of conversation is really strong, we will need words to disrupt that flow so that the truth can enter in. Below are some for you to try on. In some cases, I've added extra context so you can feel into the follow-through after the interruptive phrase. You'll see that some of these disruptors are very benign, and others more challenging. In each case, let's imagine a conversation about a joint project between yourself and another business owner. It's gone off the rails. The bolded phraseology can be adapted to lots of scenarios, but it will make the power of the language more evident to have one in mind.

Can I pause us for a minute? *I'm sensing something else in the conversation and I'd like to address it.*

I'd like to get really real here. *I think we're getting off track.*

Is anyone else noticing the elephant in the room? *I don't know why we haven't addressed how upset so-and-so is.*

Not to put a turd in the soup, *but I think our plan has failed and we need to start from scratch.*

I need to raise my hand here. *It seems to me there are some underlying issues that need to be addressed before we can keep going. We aren't going to get the results we want if we don't address ABC.*

This seems to be very upsetting. I suggest we take a breath and come back to this discussion another day. *For now, it's enough to know that things aren't working and we have some work ahead of us to sort it out.*

I'm in shock about what's been said. I'm not able to contribute to the conversation today. Excuse me.

I'm asking you to lower your voice. It's not necessary to yell for me to hear. If you lower your voice I'll be able to hear you better. If you don't lower your voice I'm going to take a break. I'm not interested in continuing this conversation like this.

Which brings us to our second topic for this chapter. Learning how to speak the truth under peaceful circumstances can be stressful. Clients who try this report feeling awkward, as if they're trying to play chess on a board where everyone else is playing checkers. Or speaking a language that is very old, that people can only vaguely understand. But after awhile it becomes part of the culture that is you. You become the person that people are relieved to be around because there is no B.S. It's worth the effort.

Notice that in the sample language above, we're not shouting our truths in that moment. This is only the interrupt that opens the space for more in-depth conversation.

LET'S FACE IT, EMOTIONS ARE CHARGED

But what about telling the truth effectively when there is excessive emotion? It's what takes an ordinary business challenge up a notch, isn't it? And because the river of life is moving quickly, many of the things we're used to have disappeared, like retirement plans, stock portfolios, not to mention the fact that we're getting older by the year. All these things add to the anxiety level in business settings. The presence of upset people, yourself and others, shouldn't surprise us.

Having soaked in a lifetime of excessive negative emotion such as anger and grief, both my own and that of those close to me, I'd like to advance a theory here. Putting aside actual psychological disorders, excessive emotion can usually be traced to a loss, or the fear of a loss, one that is too big to contain. The cork on the bottle of a pleasant personality comes flying off, and a storm comes out of the bottle. I'll say it again:

Excessive anger is usually about a loss.

Excessive grief – sobbing, for example – and other strong emotions shown in a business context are also often about a loss or the possibility of one.

Let's look at some examples and see if we can illuminate the range of this theory. The goal here is for you to be able to understand and navigate these conversations better, however, remember that you can also always just remove yourself. Leaving is an option, even if it means you lose business. It may be the best thing to happen to you.'

Inciting Incident and Emotional Response	Possible Associated Loss and Feelings
A demand for refund after the fact, angry and insulting now, in spite of no complaints during the consumption of the service. Usually a high investment.	Feeling foolish in the eyes of a family member. Labouring under self-judgment at not creating results. Feeling like a wimp for not speaking up sooner. Loss of self-respect.

Inciting Incident and Emotional Response	Possible Associated Loss and Feelings
Poor Performance on the part of a team member leading to an angry, verbally-abusive firing.	The business is under financial strain, the lack of performance adds to the pressure of going bankrupt. Feeling alone, misunderstood, like a failure. Loss of face, pride, sense of self.
A collaborative partner does not carry their weight – pent up frustration, feelings of being used, passive aggressive non-communication.	Loss of hoped-for increase in income, the joy of being simpatico with someone and the feelings of accomplishing something special. Loss of time invested. Feeling stupid.
A broken promise for a pay raise. Refusal to reconsider. Backpedalling, justifications, accusations.	Feeling cornered and put on the spot. Loss of control and authority. "I'm the boss, I decide." "It's my right to change my mind." Loss of confidence at making good decisions.
Downsizing, or change or role, leading to tantrums, little mischiefs or lack of initiative. Missed deadlines. Unfriendliness. Backstabbing and gossip.	Loss of confidence, hopes for future, as well as the more obvious losses of income, credibility and stature in the business.

As you consider these examples, add your own, or make these more your own.

Because what is the point of this reveal? Sure, understanding is lovely, but it doesn't pay the bills. It might advance me as a person, but it doesn't advance my business per se. Fair enough.

Here's where the rubber meets the road. As you pursue having better conversations in challenging circumstances, you will meet excessive emotion. Even if it's only in your imagination, you can be sure you'll run into it. The first thing is to be clear – we are not condoning bad behavior, bullying in any of its forms, or workplace violence of any kind. However, and not to put a turd in the soup here, high emotions are not always avoidable by quitting. And high emotions are there for a reason. If you choose to remain in a situation that has these challenges in it, and thousands of people do, let's have some tools to make it better.

The single tool for right now is this: a simple question to ask yourself that will help you become the rare kind of person who can safely and powerfully tell the truth:

In the face of this emotion, what is the loss this person is grappling with?

Putting it a couple of different ways may help, so here are a few nuances:

Whoa, this dude is clearly upset. Look at him go off the deep end. What is he protecting?

She's freaking right out!!! It just keeps getting worse. I don't know if I can handle this, I feel like giving in and waving the white flag, it's not worth it even if the project fails. But hang on a second … what in heck is it she thinks she's going to lose, to make her respond this way anyway?

What other ways of asking yourself this can you add? Keep it simple, the better to remember. Now, thinking back to occasions when you've faced excessive emotion, what new insight can you draw?

Remember, earlier we said it matters 'how' we tell the truth, not just 'that' we tell it. If you choose to tell the truth in the face of emotion, here are some pieces that may help. Notice that they at once protect your boundaries and speak out a degree of truth with the intention that it has a good chance of landing. Because if a truth gets spoken in a forest and it doesn't land, it really is possible that it may as well not have been spoken.

You're going to the trouble of speaking up, whether it's to an angry client or someone else, so let's make it effective.

I'm really grasping the fact that you're very upset right now. Would it be better to have this conversation another time?

Wow, your behavior is really saying something to me. This must be a big deal to you. I don't understand, but I can see that' it's a big deal for you.

Please! I need to ask you to come back to the conversation. I'm trying to understand you and I can't make sense of it.

Clearly this isn't a good time to talk. Maybe later.

Obviously there's something else going on that we aren't talking about at the moment. If you can hear me out, I have a question that might help.   What is it that's at stake here? What seems like it's in jeopardy, can you help us all understand that?

I'm finding this very difficult to follow, but I would like to offer a suggestion. Let's call it a day today, and you can take some time to write down your concerns. I'd really like to understand them well, and that might be a good way to try it.

However you put the truth in these highly-charged moments, be sure you're clear about your own boundaries. I'm unusual in this regard, as I feel it's part of my life's purpose to forge a way out of these kinds of situations, so I stick with it longer than most. I've been inoculated and wear a kind of adaptable suit of armor that serves me well. So here's a rule of thumb for you:

If you feel yourself becoming emotional as well, choose a quick but truthful exit phrase and then leave.

If you're able to be neutral enough and your boundaries feel strong, try any of the truth-telling suggestions up to three times, looking not for a complete resolution, but for a kind of understanding, or détente. If three attempts does nothing, it's probably a good idea to find your way to the exit and try again from another angle another day.

In the words of William Ury, in his The Power of the Positive No, you will be better able to operate in these scenarios with your 'yes' and your 'no' clear, like so:

YES – you want to have conflict-free dealings in business. You'll plan for it and work on it. Most of the time that will be possible.

NO – you will not put up with more than a teaspoon or cupful (you define how much) of intense, stressful emotion at the workplace. You will give it a shot, for the benefit of the business and the people involved. But you will put yourself first and be ready with your no.

In summary, you CAN handle the truth. Telling it and hearing it, even in the presence of high emotion.

"The best thing about being self-employed is that when you talk to yourself, you can call it a staff meeting."

INTERNET MEME

CHAPTER 4

Stop this Meeting

"Excuse me, could I pause you for a minute?" said I.

"Yes, sure."

"I apologize, but I am really confused. I understand what you're saying in this presentation about marketing and the importance of it, but I don't understand why we're talking about it right now."

Cue the sound of startled silence from the room of about 15 people, with about 90 minutes left on the day's agenda.

"Would it be possible to review what it is we're trying to achieve in this meeting? My understanding is that we both want to leave this meeting with confidence that we're on the right track. That when we leave this meeting and your beautiful country tomorrow, you will know what we really want to achieve, and what will make us happy. And we, on the other hand, will leave with hope and confidence that you will be able to carry that out well without us here. We really want to leave you with everything we can to make that happen, and I think there are a few things that we should say before our time runs out.

Although the marketing information is useful, we have quite a bit of experience with marketing -- actually I have nearly 10 years or so of marketing experience and I am a teacher of marketing from time to time and I know my partner also understands branding and marketing – her husband is a businessman of some repute, as you know.

Do you think it would be okay if we cover a few points here, and then if time remains we can see whether we should talk more about marketing? I really don't want us to waste the precious time we have together, with 15 smart brains around the table from around the world, and today our last day together."

Pause.

"Perhaps if we run out of time, you could send us your presentation notes, and we could review it at our leisure. If

that would be possible, I think it would be excellent to use this time for something else. What are your thoughts?"

"Sure, okay…you mean you want to hijack my presentation…" said jokingly but meaningfully, as is always the case in this kind of scenario.

"Ah, you have spent a lot of time preparing, this is true. Thank you so much. It's not that we don't value your work, I only want for us to not regret how we used our face-to-face time. The two things I think are essential to cover now, are as follows… I think if we wait to cover this by phone, it will be very challenging to have everyone be present, especially with time zone differences, and I know we all want the project, and the funds it represents, to succeed…would you agree?"

This is an edited version of a real conversation. The woman throwing the 'turd in the soup' was yours truly. From the dialogue, you can, I'm sure, gather the stakes -- the project was in fact, going downhill fast.

Have you ever been in an unproductive meeting such as this? Or even just a stultifyingly dull one?

Depending on your status in the room, it can be a relatively political act to call a stop to a conversation, and especially if there's power and authority present – i.e. you are not the big cheese – you may find it difficult to fathom even interrupting the proceedings.

But here's the thing. If you're expected to be an active participant, contribute to the conversation and the forward movement of whatever work is at hand, especially if you're a vendor being paid, your oar is needed in sync with the other rowers, otherwise you're going to impede the boat's progress. In these times of rapid hiring, firing and downsizing, if you're not with the team, you will soon find yourself off it.

Even if you don't stop the meeting, there are ways in which to influence its pace and accessibility. Be brave, and if you intuit something is amiss, try adapting one of these pieces of language:

> *"Excuse me, I hate to interrupt, but would it be possible to keep this meeting on time, or maybe even end early? I know we all want to be as productive as possible and it seems like we could wrap this up in 10 or 15 minutes."*

> *"If there isn't anything more to cover on the official agenda, can we call official time on this meeting? I'd love to squeeze in a piece of work before my next appointment."*

> *"Why don't we meet for a coffee one of these days and we can chat more? Right now I'd love to get down to business."*

> *"My time is really tight today, but I want to keep this project moving. What can we do to cut to the chase?"*

> *"I have to confess, I am totally lost. Am I the only one not*

understanding the relevance of this discussion? I thought our goal here was X. Could someone help me connect the dots? Why are we talking about Y?"

"I read somewhere that some of the most creative companies in the world keep their meetings short by making everyone stand instead of sit. Their meetings are generally less than 10 minutes long! I love that."

"I'm curious, does everyone here need to be in this meeting? Let's put some people out of their misery if we can, and at the very least they can go have a nap or something. Who here feels like they can be excused and it won't affect their productivity? And who here feels like they can be excused if they can say just 1 minute of something and then get back to work?"

Of course, if you have the influence, or are the person convening the meeting, starting out on the right foot can save a lot of angst. To save yourself from ever finding yourself in meeting purgatory, use these guidelines:

1. **Be clear about the goal of the meeting.** You and everyone attending should be able to state it simply in the form of 'The goal of this meeting is XYZ.'

2. **Review whose presence, in fact, is essential for the meeting.** Test this thoroughly by saying 'If ABC person were not at the meeting, could we still achieve our goal?"

3. **Review what information you need.** Keeping meetings small is good, but you still need all the right information. If a person can send the facts along in a brief summary, or brief another person, usually the information can be present without commandeering an actual human.

4. **Set an assertive time frame.** If you usually have meetings for an hour, and that's what people book off in their appointment books, so be it, but try for 30 minutes. Anything shorter than an hour, just as a game and a challenge.

   If your meetings double as team building, and have a brainstorming component, longer time frames can be purposeful. But don't default to thinking that every meeting needs to also be socially pleasant or ensure everyone has a good time. Practice practical time frames for practical meetings.

You can suggest this checklist for meeting planning even if you're not the convener. Citing productivity and profitability, suggest to the meeting holder that you know this checklist is useful. Then together, review, and be in cahoots during the meeting to achieve your goals of a nice, tightly-run gathering.

Of course, none of this is possible if it's unclear what the goals of the meeting are. If that part is unclear, you have another conversation at hand. (Who holds meetings where the outcome is unclear? A lot more people than we might think.)

If that's the case, go back to Chapter Two, and review the Delta Model and its three questions. Asking "Where are you now?" "Where do you want to go?" and "How do you want to get there?" for meetings is very effective, and is the model I used to call a halt to the gathering I described at the beginning of the chapter. In fact, I'd like to suggest we pause for a moment and have you flip back a few pages to reread that section. As you do so, look for the three Delta questions embedded therein, as well as the 'Yes" and 'No' from Chapter Three, and in that way you can strengthen your awareness of the tools we're accumulating in this book.

Some days you might wish, like I do, that you could just pull the fire alarm to get out of a meeting. However, after the first few times you use your own version of the above tactics well, and succeed, I think you'll find it becomes refreshing. The injection of positive energy as a result of saying NO to a poor use of time is a high we could all get used to!

A final note. If you're in a meeting that's not productive, you are complicit by not pausing it, or putting a stop to it. Your presence says that you're okay with it. Are you? If not, and you're looking for an alternative to a conversation about it?

Leave.

Go ahead, imagine it, then give it a try at your first low-stakes opportunity. Feign surprise if someone tries to stop you. Oh, are you needed? It seemed pretty clear not…and there's work waiting.

There's more than one way to get your message across. You might be surprised that the world doesn't come to an end.

Stopped meetings represent a claiming back of that one commodity that no-one, from office assistants to billionaires, can get more of—time.

Unless, of course, we all start putting a stop to more meetings.

*"This is your world. Shape it
or someone else will."*

GARY LEW

CHAPTER 5

Hiring, Performance Reviews & Firing

As soon as you have a single assistant, congratulations, you now have a team! You are the leader, the big cheese, the grand poo-bah! And with it come conversations that may be uncomfortable, simply because you've never had them before. However, with a little help, the right conversations can set you up for success.

Here are some of the most common stumbling points and the corresponding language to try:

HIRING

What? How is hiring a challenging business conversation, Andrea? You're right, this is usually a happy and relatively easy interaction, but there are a few key points that, inserted here, will make future interactions easier. So let's be proactive about it, why don't we?

> *"Let's try you out on this compensation for the first 30 days, then have a review to see how it's going. At that point, if things are going the way we hope, I foresee being able to move your pay up. If not though, we can discuss it then and go from there."*

> *"I'd like to give this role a try for the next 90 days. I know it's not a long time, but it's a new role and I'm not entirely sure how it will work out. If that's not doable for you, I understand, but if you're interested in trying it out, I'll send you the contract for 90 days and we can get going."*

As you can no doubt surmise, the main takeaway here is to hire with an 'out' clause for yourself. There are a lot of new factors in any hire: the person is new, the role may be new, it may be new to you to have this kind of team member. All of the risk in this newness is easily mitigated by giving yourself a timeframe in which to assess. Don't be afraid to assign a new time frame after the first review, and again until your confidence level is where you'd like it to be. This applies equally when it's a competitive market and good people are hard to find. You can be gung-ho and sell the benefits of working with you hard. Just also be sure to set the expectations from the beginning, and at the very least, make it easy to schedule a performance review.

PERFORMANCE REVIEWS & FIRING

Firing, on the other hand, can be a sticky situation. Why else are there so many firms that specialize in doing the deed for you, and movies made about it? In this case, integrating performance reviews into the communication, giving clear expectations and setting time frames are the elements to bear in mind:

> *"Based on the results from last month, it looks like this is the second month the job didn't get done. Is everything alright with you? Is there something you need from me to get it done next month?"*

> *"I want to make it really clear what needs to change. Where the last two months, XYZ has been happening, I need ABC to happen instead. Where DEF is happening, we can't let that happen again. I need to know if you understand that, and can take responsibility for GHI to happen instead."*

> *"Okay so with that clarity, I'm going to give us this next month to see how things go. Let's meet again 30 days from now to review. But if anything comes up beforehand that you need help with, don't wait, find me. If we don't*

have a change here when we meet, it's going to be really hard to do anything but ask you to leave. Does that make sense? Fair enough?"

Bonus points if you noticed the Delta Model, our universal key for difficult conversations, making its presence known here -- and not for the last time.

Just another word about firing. I've discovered that business owners have an extremely high tolerance for poor performance when faced with needing to fire someone. It's amazing what they'll put up with to avoid saying the words 'You're fired!' I guess not everyone has Donald Trump's constitution.

Not that I get excited and happy about terminating people, or the chaos that comes with it as the organization (and the person) adjusts. It's definitely a less than optimal occasion, unplanned and a symbol of something hopeful just not working out somehow. But as we'll say more of in a later chapter about graceful goodbyes, right now, I'd like for you to embrace reality. You will fire a number of people in your career as a business person. Without question, it is going to come up, just like, let's say, funerals happen in life, or dates that don't lead to marriage. So let's build up your resilience towards it. I hope that knowing you'll need to fire people at some point in your future will normalize it for you and you'll feel more at peace when the moment arrives.

For what it's worth, here's a funny story for the road, about firing:

The day I took up my first General Manager position I was in for a big surprise. My first task, assigned by my boss and mentor, was to tell the General Manager – the one I'd be replacing - that he had been let go. (This was totally uncalled for yet characteristic of Thomas, who I know knew exactly how badly he was passing the buck!)

The person was a total dear, too. He had helped me come into the organization, which I will bless him for until my last day on earth. On top of that, he was on vacation when I got the promotion and had no idea what he was coming back to.

In spite of all that, the task was assigned to me, and I'm quite sure I bungled it mightily, squirming, having nothing to go on, much less a performance review. I probably did my best imitation of a polite Asian person and apologized, for who knows what. I hope he took it up with Thomas later, but whew, that was the last I heard of it.

Suffice to say, sometimes you have to show your teeth a little, and fire someone for good reasons. Maybe Thomas had a good reason, who knows? But it sure gave me an experience of firing that's served me well. It doesn't scare me anymore and nor should it you.

A tree 'fires' its leaves every autumn, and a mother bird 'fires' its babies from the nest in spring, right? Be alert to the need to call an end to a relationship within your business, and if it's your turn to fire, do it swiftly.

"Do no harm, but take no shit."

UNKNOWN

CHAPTER 6
Collections & Refund Requests

When a farmer ploughs a new field, boldly planting something where no one has dreamed of planting before, she expects to encounter some rocks. Your business, serving in the way it does in the world, the way only you can, is going to encounter refunds and collections.

Each one of these topics can lead to some particularly thorny business conversations. Be proactive in these areas, and it will pay you in real cash and avoid the loss of morale that can leach perfectly good energy needed to grow the good things.

SPEAK NOW TO AVOID COLLECTIONS LATER

Collections, or making effort in order to get paid your fees because the client hasn't voluntarily paid when agreed, is a process that can usually be avoided if you take a few preparatory steps, which will require a few decisions from you.

STEP 1. Where possible, collect payment, partial or all, before your work begins.

Industry convention may prevent you from this, however there is nothing to keep you from trying, particularly if the work you do commands a higher fee, or takes place over time, as opposed to being completed right away.

For example, it makes sense for a construction company, about to renovate your entire home, to say,

"We require a 25% deposit to start our work."

It might feel quite different coming from a window washer who'll be done in a few hours. On the other hand, if you're the window washing company and you'll be doing the windows every two weeks, you could float the idea of prepayment, since you're counting on that business.

Think of this as sharing the risk inherent in any exchange. If you're risking something in committing to the work, you have at least a passing chance at seeking payment up front. New industries and services pop up all the time, and new standards too. If you get push back, be ready to be flexible, but have your reasons for collecting something up front prepared.

STEP 2. Document the payment schedule and be sure to include appropriate terms. You may be interested in the bolded parts of the sample in particular:

"We're excited to begin working together to achieve your goals! The following is the payment schedule for the package you've selected:

25% of total fees due to kick start the work.

As soon as payment is received, *we will send you the orientation materials, intake forms and schedule you for your initial assessment, which as discussed,* ***we hope can be next week.***

3 payments of 25% every 30 days, to be paid automatically via the credit card of your choice.

*Or, if you prefer, **full payment of fees can be made up front, with a 5% discount applicable.***

*Note: In the case of the 4-payment plan, you will receive a courtesy reminder in case payment is not made on the due date. If payment is not made within 5 days of the due date, **a penalty of $100 per late payment will be charged to cover administrative costs.***

If your credit card number has changed, please follow the instructions in the reminder to make that change. If you require additional support at any time, we'd be glad to help! Write to us via email at emailaddress@ yourcompany.com or call 1-888-YOURNUMBER.

*You'll find my signature below to make this agreement official, NAME. My assistant is standing by to **receive your countersign,** and help in any other way. I look forward **to getting going with you next week!***

While your specifics may be different, the principles of the leverage points in a well set-up agreement like this apply. The client wants something from you and you are ready to provide it. The act of them paying is the flick of the switch that begins work.

When that payment isn't made, you wait. Do not provide services. Until the first payment is collected, the sale isn't final. Technically, you haven't been hired yet.

This may seem elementary, but for newer business owners, it can be a gray area. Do not succumb to the temptation to 'just get started, payment is on its way.' Even old-timers in business sometimes slip, particularly when it comes to doing business with friends, or long-time former clients. This is a slippery slope toward where statistics show the most intense collections action happening – in courtrooms. Just like car accidents happening within a few blocks of home, familiarity breeds laziness. Don't do it.

If you set a precedent that you're a softie in this regard, be ready for at least a few collections headaches in your future.

STEP 3. Automate the first part of your after-the-fact collections process.

Using the tools available to you, like email autoresponders that are triggered by non payment of an invoice such as a credit card being declined, a calendar reminder that an invoice is overdue, or a human being such as a bookkeeper sending you a report that shows who's missed a payment, setting up an automated sequence of communications to help you collect payment is quite easy. In all cases, adapt for the right tone of your organization, being sure to customize for your values.

First communication sample:

Dear Name,

We noticed that your payment in the amount of $_____ due on _____, was declined/ rejected/not made. Unfortunately, it is now overdue.

To prevent disruption in service that could have consequences for you beyond our control, we ask that you take care of payment in the next 7 days. You can do so using any of these options:

Option #1:
Use this link to make payment now: LINK
You can also change credit cards at this link if that is desired.

Option #2:
Email us at emailaddress@yourcompany.com and let us know how we can support an alternative means of payment.

continued next page

---

continued from previous page

NAME, we look forward to hearing from you via one of the options. It continues to be a pleasure and privilege to work with you!

SIGNATURE

Second communication sample, 2 days before the deadline expressed in above:

NAME,

We haven't heard from you regarding payment of the overdue balance, $_____. Below is a copy of our first notice regarding this.

Travel, busy seasons, and even email delivery can sometimes cause a lapse in communication, so we're sending a courtesy reminder. Please help ensure that we can continue our work together by taking care of payment immediately.

LINK

continued next page

continued from previous page

If there is a problem of some kind, communicating with us at EMAIL ADDRESS allows us to work with you to resolve this. If we don't hear from you by the end of business tomorrow, we will take further action to collect payment and in certain cases, services will need to be suspended.

We will also leave this information at your phone number and look forward to the easy resolution of this with your partnership.

SIGNATURE

Third communication sample, within up to 7 days after the deadline cited above:

Dear Name,

Unfortunately, we have not heard from you regarding the outstanding balance of $_____$ for services rendered. Effective immediately, we will be suspending service and (insert other consequences and actions that will be taken, such as:

continued next page

continued from previous page

- your membership in our groups removed
- your website shut down
- your coaching appointments cancelled
- our team's work on your file stopped
- your materials removed from our promotions
- your passwords changed
- access to your files removed

Once we've heard from you, and payment is made, we will gladly be open to restoring these things.

Also, in due course, due to the size of the outstanding balance, we will be pursuing further action through a collections agency and/or legal assistance. Should you wish to prevent this from happening, we recommend you be in touch with us at your earliest convenience.

SIGNATURE

Collections is never a fun matter. At heart, it's a breach of contract that, if you accept it, sets a crucial precedent that can destroy companies. If a person is communicating with you in good faith and has difficulty paying, you may choose to set new terms for payment, however these should be made official and documented with deadline dates and penalties, i.e. the equivalent of interest payments levied. Being willing to allow payments beyond the original agreement is plenty of goodwill. Don't make the mistake of being soft on terms or not documenting this the second time around or it will lead to a third, and the likelihood of not being paid will only grow.

STEP 4.   Move quickly into relationship-based conversation to hopefully collect.

The ideal result of the above samples, showing just one route communication can take, is that if payment isn't made, at least the lines of communication are opened. You receive word from the client-in-the-balance. Something perfectly reasonable has happened, or the client is in a bit of a stuck place, but payment is forthcoming. It's just a matter of a little time.

As a smaller business, I support you in working with clients rather than incurring legal costs if the dollar amount warrants. Still, make some effort to put teeth into your new agreement. If you don't, and it becomes easy for the client to ask for new terms again, you'll get caught in a cycle that is wasteful and draining, not to mention negatively impacts your ability to do great work together.

Here is a template for recapping the agreement that is firm, but doesn't have you in overreaction mode.

Dear NAME,

Thank you for our discussion regarding payment of the overdue invoice #_____ in the amount of $_____. I appreciate you reaching out so we can come to new terms and an agreement to take care of this.

Based on our conversation, I'm documenting for our records that you will make payment of the above amount as follows:

3 Payments of $_____ on (date), (date) and (date.)

Payment will be made using the credit card on file, and you have authorized us to run that on the dates above, including the first one by the end of this week. Because of the additional administrative costs involved, we will be billing you an extra $30 per payment, for a total of $90 that will be added to the first payment on (date.)

NAME, although we agreed that this should take care of the amount outstanding, I would like to

continued next page

continued from previous page

> express my hope that if you should be able to render payment earlier than the above, you be in touch with us right away.
>
> Should a payment not go through per this agreement, you have agreed that you will take whatever actions necessary to avoid further collections action.
>
> Meanwhile, we will resume work in good faith,
>
> SIGNATURE

STEP 5. As a final resort, calculate the cost-benefits, and if you decide it's worth it, use the appropriate legal process to raise the stakes. Stay agile and detached.

The sample language I've used here has its limitations, however I hope you'll take the structure and adapt it as necessary. Where you see leverage being applied, apply what you can. You may feel less assertive than the sample language, or you may feel more aggressive. Take the route that fits. And, if the amount being collected doesn't seem worth the effort, you may be right. You can write this off as bad debt. Take the action that fits the dollar amount.

If you decide to take further legal action, there are a plethora of services that will be glad to help you, payable on the percentage or for fee.

APPLYING THE DELTA MODEL THROUGHOUT

Meanwhile, a final note here regarding every step of this process. Awkwardness and even outright tension or volatility are very possible in these conversations. This is why prevention is worth it from the start. When you're in these tough conversations, however, remember that no one is going to failsafe the viability of your business more than you. You are the proverbial mamma or papa bear, and your business and its vision are your cubs. Use the three Delta questions as your North Star and you'll never be far from being able to have these conversations.

Here is an example of a phone conversation that leads to the recapping of terms above:

"Hi Name, good to be in communication." (Where are we now?)

"Yes, same. And, I'm sorry for the payment problem." (Where are we now?)

"I appreciate that. What are you thinking about resolving things? (Where would you like to go? Obviously you know where you would like to go – you'd like payment.)

"I've run into a tight spot and I can't make a full payment right now. But I can offer to pay a third by the end of the week, and then the remainder in two payments next month." (Where would you like to go?)

"Gotcha, so that would mean…. (repeat what was offered, but do the actual math and make notes so it's explicit.)" (You'd like to go here, is that right?)

"Yes."

"I think that can work. I'd like to make sure this doesn't drag out too long, if you're able to pay the balance off sooner than this, would you reach out to me?" (Is there wiggle room on where you'd like to go, closer to where I'd like to go?)

"Sure, I can do that. I'm not sure if I will be able to but I can let you know if I can."

"Okay. I know things can happen and I'm willing to help out. Because of the extra administrative charges involved, I need to add a $30 charge for each payment. That's a $90 total that I'd like to be paid this week along with the first payment. Given the extra time we're looking at for the rest of the payments, does that sound fair enough?" (A wrinkle in where I'd like to go, as a condition for where you're asking to go.)

"I understand. Yes, that sounds reasonable enough."

"Alright, well I think that does it. The last details is around actual payment. We have your credit card on file as per our prior agreement. Shall we bill you $_____ on Friday this week, and then again on (date) and (date?)" (How would you like to get there?)

"Yes, Friday afternoon please. Also when can we get our _____ restored? We're going to need that to keep going with things."

"Once the payment on Friday is made, we can restore that for you, no problem. What I'll also do is document this conversation and sign it so that you have that assurance about these new terms. I'll have it sent over for you to review and countersign. It's Wednesday today, so, by end of business Friday everything should be back to normal." (How would you like to get there?)

"Good. Thanks and sorry for this."

"Glad we could help."

REFUNDS

Compared with collections, refunds are a somewhat easier process to navigate – however, depending on how new you are in business, and your personality, refunds can hit close to your heart. A client of yours isn't happy for some reason. It can sting.

A bit of aloe vera for that is some wisdom gained from experience:

The more careful you are about your growth, and the more steadily but slowly you bring on new business, the less risk of refunds you're going to incur.

The faster and more leveraged your growth is, in other words, the more new clients you bring on faster, the more refund requests you're going to experience.

It's the nature of numbers and intimacy. If you're desiring bigger growth, enjoy it! And know that some percentage of refund requests come with the territory. Your marketing is casting a wider net in order to catch more fish, and the number of dud cans you catch in there is just the price of business. There's no such thing as a no-refund bigger business.

When you're smaller, it's still possible for someone to become unhappy, however you will likely know about it long before a refund request comes in. Being proactive, you will either fix it or offer a refund or alternative before it becomes a request. That is the difference.

Here is some language to illustrate how a refund request can occur, to better inoculate you, and perhaps give you a laugh – which is the best medicine for what can be trying, if you let it be personal.

Refund Request Samples:

"I need the money back, I have to get groceries, please refund."

"I used your product and it wasn't what I expected. It was _____ (description of how it wasn't a fit) _____ and you might want to think about fixing all that. I expect a full refund and unfortunately I won't get my time wasted back but I guess that is the price of doing business."

"I can't believe how terrible your company is. You obviously couldn't care less about anything other than making a buck, and the way you treat your customers is nothing short of brutal. I have no idea why anyone does business with you ever and you can bet I will be telling the WORLD how horrible you are. If I don't get a full refund IMMEDIATELY I will report you to the police."

"After much consideration, I would like a refund for the program I took with you from last year. I thought it was good at the time, and I know I participated in it, but after thinking about it a lot the last 12 months, I realize it was the wrong thing for me. I shouldn't have signed up for it. I'm ashamed of my decision and I want to make it right for my family who made sacrifices for the investment I made."

"Refund me. Didn't like."

"This just isn't working. I don't like the work you're doing and you're doing more harm than good. I think we should call it quits and cancel our agreement. I don't expect a full refund, but I would consider meeting you half way and of course, cancelling now, I expect not to be charged the remaining fees."

And here is some language you can used when faced with a refund request, with different options for different circumstances:

Dear Name,

Thank you for your request for a refund for (name of product or service.) We would like to first of all acknowledge that you weren't satisfied with what you received and we greatly appreciate you letting us know so we could have the opportunity to do everything we can to address it. *(Where you are now. Acknowledging where they are now.)*

Specifically concerning your refund request, I clearly understand what you're asking, and *(Insert your response... where you're willing to go. Either you will refund them, you won't, or something in between. A few examples in bullets below.)*

continued next page

continued from previous page

- "Because your request falls inside our 30-day refund timeframe, I would be happy to issue you a full refund. Please be on the look out for an email confirmation. In our experience, you can expect your credit card statement to reflect the refund within 3-5 business days."

- "Although we have a no refund policy, I have confirmed that the errors/issues/problems you described. This is not the kind of experience we want our clients to have, so I would like to refund your purchase in full along with a gift of a $20 Amazon.com gift certificate/ a $20 donation to (insert charity) in your name/ a $20 credit towards a future product of ours. This is just a small token of appreciation for the inconvenience /less than perfect experience you had.

- "It looks like there must be a misunderstanding. During the course of the service, we received several confirmations from you that you were excited and pleased. We have a no-refund policy for this service, however, even if we did, you would definitely be outside the time

continued next page

continued from previous page

frame. Regrettably, we won't be able to issue you a refund, however I'm open to hearing if there is another way we can make things better."

- "Really get how upset you are. We're not in business to create upset customers so this is very upsetting for us too. You invested a lot into the work, and so did we, so I hope that something can be done here. NAME, because your request is coming after our refund timeframe has expired, we can't issue you a refund in all fairness to our other clients. Although it's not what you were hoping for, is there some other way in which we might help matters?"

- "You're obviously extremely upset. Clearly, we're not in business to create upset customers, and I regret that this has happened. Our services come with costs that cannot be refunded, and because we in fact worked overtime to deliver to the specifications you gave us, unfortunately we can't process your request. We understand that you may use your influence to tell other people about the experience from your point of view,

continued next page

continued from previous page

and while we wish we could make it better, we feel that we've been more than fair. To make an exception with a refund in this case would set a precedent that isn't a fit for our team culture. Our people did great work and we will stand by them and the work in public if need be. Given time, we hope that the good work that was done will prove to be of value to you. We wish you all the best, NAME, in your good work in the world."

- "Wow, your comments really hit home. I appreciate your feedback and although we don't ordinarily do refunds, you've given me some real food for thought that I think is going to help us improve greatly and I would like to make an exception. Based on the fact that about 50% of your fees were spent on costs to serve you, I would like to offer you a 40% refund. If this would suit you, I can make the logistics happen *(insert details.)*

- "I hear you. I agree that things are not working out and would be glad to officially call an end to our work as of today. I will be happy to consider this email a cancellation and we will stop billing you effective today."

And with that, I hope you feel much more equipped to have these inevitable conversations, kindly. Now that you know the notes to play, you can also make up your own tunes. The above examples are just some places to start.

"To err is human, to forgive, divine."

ALEXANDER POPE

CHAPTER 7
Apologizing

It was summer of 1992, and after driving 250 miles - dodging a speeding ticket to get from New York to Toronto in time - I arrived at the reception desk slightly breathless, clutching my piece of paper.

"Hi, my name is Andrea, and I'm here for my interview for the JET Programme."

"Oh hi, Andrea. Let me see. Hmm….I don't see your name here. What position are you applying for?"

"Coordinator of International Relations."

"Oh! Okay, let me just check on something. May I have your sheet of paper?"

"Sure."

"Ahhhh....I see the problem. Your appointment isn't until tomorrow. All the CIR appointments are happening tomorrow."

"What? Oh my goodness. Wait, no, see on my appointment letter? It says today's date."

"It does? It can't be. Hang on. You're right. Well, you're half right. It says today's date, the 26th, but it also says Friday, which is tomorrow! Alright, please have a seat. I will look into this."

So went the conversation at the scene of what, in my young life, was a turning point. Would I get the job working for the Japanese government, where I hoped I would launch my career in international relations, perhaps reaching that pinnacle of translator for the United Nations, or something else unimaginably exciting to me then?

Little did I know then, that yes, not only would I get that job, but I would meet my husband-to-be and get engaged within 6 weeks of stepping foot in Japan. Or, that the job would shape so much of the rest of my life, including this book.

My life has owed a lot to apologies, and as a result, I have a particular affinity for them, and having them well. The story above concludes with an apology that I will share with you in a moment. But first, let's acknowledge apologizing as the vast topic it is.

APOLOGIES ARE DOORWAYS TO RELIEF AND GOOD ENERGY

If there's one sweeping thing to be said about apologies, it's that they are tolerations. Things that too many of us tolerate for far too long. Until uttered, they are one of the most anxiety-causing things in life, and unspoken apologies or regret in business can drain cash flow in a heartbeat.

A first step in addressing this challenge is to ask you the simple question 'Where are you putting up with things that you could apologize for?'

Examples could be:

- regret about the way you handled something with a team member
- not fulfilling a promise to a joint venture partner
- working late (again) and disappointing your family
- providing less than great service to a client,
- letting yourself down in some way,
- or any number of other things.

Simply acknowledging these possibilities can release trapped energy.

APOLOGIES ARE OPPORTUNITIES

For better or for worse, many people associate apologies with shame or great difficulty, and personal sacrifice. To apologize in business can be seen as 'falling on one's sword' and we're often cautioned not to apologize – even if we know we ought to – lest we take too much responsibility and therefore come under fire. "If you apologize, you might have to refund money to the client." Or "An apology shows weakness, and opens you up to legal action."

While this may be true in some cases, I have found that not taking responsibility, not making things right, and not apologizing can have much more far-reaching effects.

If you can't apologize, it's very difficult to forgive yourself. And it's even more difficult to feel good. Apologizing (and having your apology be heard and accepted) is an opportunity to feel good.

HOW TO ACCESS THE FIRST WORDS

Big or small, what I hear often is that it's difficult to find the words to say 'I'm sorry.' Fair enough. Let's try it from a different angle. What if, in whatever situation you're in, instead of asking 'How do I say I'm sorry?' you ask instead 'What am I grateful for?'

You've just heard that a really important client received their packages from you. They arrived unusable and the client is greatly inconvenienced. She'd like to know what you're going to do about it.

If it's easy for you to say "I'm so sorry, I will make it right," that's fine.

When the words don't come easily, try acknowledging the emotions first. These might be humiliation, embarrassment, fear, or even outrage. Once these have had a chance to settle, give this slightly different question a try:

'What am I grateful for?'

Could it be that you can access gratitude for the client reaching out to tell you about the disaster (because it would be worse to find out from someone else?) Or something else? Gratitude can be the doorway to saying what's real, and if that's an apology, terrific.

FROM GRATITUDE, CONNECTION GROWS

What we may not realize when we don't apologize, is that we're actually holding our own selves hostage. You'd think that the person who would suffer most is the person who's still waiting for your apology. In my experience, that's not true. That person has a number of avenues to pursue in order to move on.

In fact, it's you, the person who hasn't spoken the apology who tends to suffer most. Learning to apologize has everything to do with forgiving yourself, and becoming gentler and more compassionate with yourself. That's the softening we're looking for. It's the softening that turns apologies from challenges into opportunities.

Let's do at least one example:

Dear NAME,

Thank you so much for reaching out to let me know you were disappointed in the CD set. I really regret that you had a poor experience with us AND I really appreciate hearing about it!

What I'd love to do is to refund your purchase in full, since it's clear that it was not a fit. I'm grateful for your specific feedback since it allows me to reflect on how we can improve this for future clients. I would not want anyone else to have the experience you had.

continued next page

continued from previous page

Would you let me know if there's something else I can do to create lemonade from this for you? If the other CDs worked fine, it would be my pleasure if you would pass them along, or, keep them for your use. And if there's something else we can do to assist you in future, NAME, don't hesitate to let us know.

Best wishes,

Name

GOOD APOLOGIES CHANGE LIVES

"Mr. and Mrs. Selection Committee, I am so grateful to you for seeing me today, in spite of the fact that there was confusion regarding the day of the appointment. For the inconvenience I'm causing you at the end of your long day of interviews, I am very sorry."

In my best Japanese, fresh from a year of intensive study, I knew I nailed my opening gambit at this all-important interview.

The interview, infused as it was with this display of apologizing prowess, went spectacularly well. And the truth is, *I was exceptionally grateful*. And regretful. And hopeful. After saying my tidily prepared words, I was relieved and ready for anything.

On the other hand, had I not been able to access, or find the words for, the apology in the way I did? Grumpily hoping they wouldn't hold the calendaring issue against me, I know the interview would not have gone over nearly as well, and, who knows where I'd be today? Besides, apologizing in the Japanese culture can be fun. No doubt that's where much of the inspiration for my thoughts and work with apologies comes from. I'm sure there will be more to say on this big topic in future.

FEWER APOLOGIES, MORE LAWSUITS?

In Japan, apologizing is actually considered not a shameful act, but a virtue. A well-expressed apology demonstrates a person's maturity and good citizenship. Instead of looking to blame others, the idea is to take more than one's share of responsibility, so that as a community or nationality, the issue is more than covered. And correspondingly, forgiveness is given more freely and easily. Could this be the reason why per capita, there are much fewer law suits and court cases, when compared with North America?

As you try on the idea of apologies as opportunities, remember. Getting right with our apologies, and cultivating a clean slate, where you have few if any unspoken apologies on your conscience, can be an energizing and cathartic act. I like to think of it as prescribing fibre for what's blocking a business, or a quarterly commitment, like New Year's Resolutions.

What unspoken apologies are you putting up with that you'd be willing to unstick? Do you have apologies you wish you could receive, as well as give? Start today by noticing both of these, and the energy they take up in your life.

Section II
Creating the Future

"Let us not disrespect – or underestimate – the power of a single great idea, well monetized, to change the world."

.ANDREA LEE

CHAPTER 8
Deal-Making & How to Share the Money

When it comes to doing business online, it is only a matter of time before you start to seek out, and build relationships with, others with whom to joint venture. What do I mean by a joint venture, exactly? For the purposes of this chapter, doing a joint venture just means doing a finite project of some kind with someone else.

With the right joint venture partners, success can become quicker and easier in some ways. The trick is how to find the right ones, and then once found, how to negotiate a deal that works.

The single biggest challenge in the joint venturing process is having the conversation about sharing the money. Oh, the number of deals that have fallen through because this part didn't work out!

Think about it.   Even if everything else is set up well - including the offer itself, the promotional copy, the schedule of the announcement, the follow-through calls, etc. -- if you haven't properly broached the topic of how the money will be shared, the potential for a falling out is big.

You know it to be true, I'm sure. Even when it comes to talking about specifics of money with your significant other, things can get heated fast.

So what's an easy way for you to be able to talk about money to a near-stranger? A way that takes the emotions and sensitivity out of the picture for both of you, and reliably allow you to come to a happy agreement?

Let me share with you a method I've used over the years.

This, quite simply, is the backbone of the 'Sharing the Money' formula. It can be flexed to adapt to different situations, but at heart, that's all there is.

So what does all this mean?

We start with some basic assumptions. As your joint venture projects get more complex, you will refine these assumptions. But for the majority of initial joint ventures, this will be a reliable place to start.

ASSUMPTION #1: There are at least four major components to any given joint venture.

- Content
- Delivery
- Marketing
- Administration/Customer Service

ASSUMPTION #2: It's helpful to assign a 'weight' to each of these components.

Our basic starting point is: Content, Delivery and Marketing are essentially equally important. Administration, including customer service and credit card processing costs, etc. take up a smaller portion of the project.

For these reasons, we use the following 'weighting' as a rule of thumb:

- 10% of the project will be assigned to Administration/ Customer Service

Of the remaining 90%, we will assign 30% each to Content, Delivery and Marketing. Which brings us back to the fundamental formula: 30 (Content) + 30 (Delivery) + 30 (Marketing) + 10 (Administration).

Make sense? Let's apply this to a sample conversation and then extrapolate to some additional thoughts.

A SAMPLE CONVERSATION: 30 + 30 + 30 + 10

In the following scenario, I have a three-week teleclass program that I'd like my new joint venture partner Jim to announce to his list. Here is an example of how the conversation might go.

Andrea: "So Jim, I'd like to talk about how we'd share the revenue we earn when you promote this program for me next month. Is this a good time for you?"

Jim: "Sure!"

Andrea: "Great. So let me tell you what I was thinking, and you can see what you think. I'm totally open to adjusting and so on, but thought it would be a good idea to start somewhere..."

Jim: "Sounds fine to me."

Andrea: "Okay, so first I wanted to break down the joint venture into elements. The way I see it, there are four main pieces we're dealing with: The content of the program itself; the delivery of the classes; the marketing of the program and then finally the administrative pieces, like customer service inquiries, the shopping cart setup, setting up the web page, and a little bit of writing the copy for the promotion. Oh and yes, I include credit card charges and so on in the administrative part. Does that seem to make sense?"

Jim: "Yes."

Andrea: "Can you think of any other elements that aren't covered by those four?"

Jim: "No, I can't, but I might later."

Andrea: "Okay, sure. When something comes up, just holler and we can insert that element into the calculations then, sound good?"

Jim: "Sounds good."

Andrea: "So based on those four elements, what made sense to me was to set aside 10% of the gross revenue to cover administrative costs. So that's 3-4% for the credit card processing and shopping cart costs. And then about 5% just to cover costs of my Virtual Assistant to help out with inquiries, customer service, etc. And then, for the remaining 90%, it seemed simple and reasonable to split that into three, giving the content, delivery and marketing equal weight. So that means allocating the revenue so that...

The Content of the program gets 30%...

The Delivery of the program gets 30%...

And then the Marketing of the program gets the final 30%.

Because each of these three pieces is essential to our success. What do you think?"

Jim: "It sounds good to me!"

Andrea: "Cool! So based on that then I figured we'd split up what we each bring to the table and from there we can come up with the actual split of the money. So...

For Content, I'll be using our materials, so that category goes to me...30%...

For Delivery, since there are 3 classes, and Jim you will be leading one of them as guest...let's give you 10% and me 20% for delivery...

Then for Marketing, you and I will both be marketing this one to our databases, so I think it's only fair to have us split this element...so 15% to you and 15% to me.

And of course I don't want to have you have to manage the administration, so we'll take care of that and associate costs here...10%...

So let's see, this works out to 25% going to you, and 75% to me. What do you think?"

Jim: "Well...I think it sounds great. The only thing I think I'd comment on is that my database is much bigger than yours. So I think the marketing might want to be adjusted to reflect that."

Andrea: "That's a good point. Your database is actually almost twice as big as mine. Hmm. Well, would you be willing to commit to sending out at least 2 solo emails to your database before the deadline we set? Because if that's the case, I would be happy to split the marketing say 20%-10%...so you get twice as much as me in that category."

Jim: "Sounds good. Yes, I'll send out one email announcing the program, and then a second email reminding them to sign up. So does that make the final split 70%-30%?"

Andrea: "Yep. So because the program is $100 per person, you'll earn $30 for each person that signs up. We have 100 slots, and if you fill even 50 of those slots, that's $1500. I'll be able to write that check or PayPal you that amount, at the end of the month...does that work?"

Jim: "Yes, that's good. I'd like it by check to avoid the PayPal costs. And then afterwards, are you going to be selling the recording? I'd love to sell that too, on an ongoing basis at the same rate..."

Andrea: "That sounds awesome. Okay! So I'll just type up a quickie email note to reflect this, and then get back to you with the promotional copy and so on that you can adapt for the initial announcement. Thanks so much Jim, I'm really excited about providing terrific value to your readers."

Jim: "Good stuff. Next time let's chat about a new launch I'm planning...we can do this again."

Andrea: "Bye for now Jim."

Jim: "Bye."

Congratulations – you now have a conversational structure you can use as a place to start as you explore joint venture territory.

Based on hundreds of these kinds of conversations, let me assure you that when it comes time for you to have this conversation, for the most part it will be just that simple.

Now here are a few additional thoughts. Remember the Money Formula isn't carved in stone, it's a tool that you can adapt.

1. There are four 'categories' or 'elements' in the above sample conversation. These are variable according to your needs. So for example, if your joint project involves programming, equipment rental, or something else, add elements to the list and divide your 30, 30, 30 and 10 accordingly. As you do so, remember you are assigning a relative 'weight' of importance to each element.

2. Sometimes you may joint venture with someone you are willing to 'lose' money on. For example, if Oprah Winfrey were to call and say 'I'd like to announce your 3-week teleseminar, Andrea,' I would do the above calculation for my own benefit, and then,

knowing those numbers, I might say something like, 'Awesome Oprah, I'd be happy to send you 90% of all revenue, keeping just 10% for my own costs.' Or not.

You might be willing to give her 100%. And in fact, that's probably not a bad business decision.

The point being, however, that you yourself understand the breakdown behind the scenes, and therefore know what you are investing into the agreement.

This is the only way you can consciously acknowledge 'why' the relationship benefits you. Oprah announcing my teleseminar could bring me so much benefit that I'm willing to 'lose' money on the initial step. (Unlikely as it is that Oprah's doing it for the money I would send her in any case!)

3. Sometimes your joint venture project may involve one-time costs up front.

For example, you may decide to co-author a Multimedia Work- book. Such a project requires an investment in graphic design for the cover, manufacturing the CDs or DVDs, etc.

What I suggest you do is negotiate these one-time costs separately. Usually an easy way to go about it is to calculate according to the above sample dialogue, and then add one thing:

"So once our initial $1500 in graphic and multimedia costs are covered by the first sales, we'll begin splitting the revenue 30/70."

That's all there is to it...

So there you have a very simple, robust method to frame your discussions about sharing the money in the joint ventures you pursue. The thing to remember here is that this is a scalable, flexible model. Use it for its key benefits which are, by way of review:

- To facilitate a straightforward conversation about money.
- To take the emotion out of the equation.
- To get buy-in from the joint venture partner as to the 'logic'
  behind the decisions at each step of the way.

SOME FINAL THOUGHTS

Oftentimes as you become well-known in your niche market, you will begin to be approached to speak, or present, or teach classes for others. These others, not knowing this method, or being very clear about how to negotiate a revenue share, will often throw out a number that they 'always' use, that actually does you a disservice. The potential partner may even say things like,

"Well, so-and-so has been teaching his program with us for this long, and he's always taken 20%."

Instead of simply bowing to this number, I invite you to try a conversation like the above, and see where you can get. When presented with a rationale in this way, most of the time the numbers start to make more sense and reflect the real value you bring to the table... Because at heart, that's what the 'Sharing the Money' conversation is about, in my opinion...coming to see where your value lies in any given situation, and making sure you leave the negotiating table with a share of the money that feels right and sits right to you and your accountant at month end.

As you practice this conversation, you will become more at ease with it, and may even surprise yourself at how sophisticated a money negotiation you can handle with peace of mind.

Now, go forth, make some deals, and share money already!

"Forget safety. Live where you fear to live. Destroy your reputation. Be notorious."

RUMI

CHAPTER 9

Asking for the Business

The sales conversation, or, asking for the business, is at the heart of what we call 'business.'

There are lots of other things that make up a business, but without selling, there is no business; you might as well throw in the towel right now. Regardless of whether it's getting one client, selling to a large group, or submitting a proposal for a contract that leads to a record income this year, selling is what makes a business a business.

Having said that, you would think asking for the business would fall into a category of something to be enthusiastic about. But for the vast majority of people, it doesn't. The conversation it takes to make a sale can sound like a fiery pit in Dante's Inferno based on some of the descriptions I've heard. And now that clients have more choices than ever, and easy ways to find them on the Internet, using review services like Yelp.com and more, the chance to bring aboard a new client can come and go very quickly. Each time this happens, the business burns money, and that can't happen for too long before real trouble comes a-knocking.

As with many of the chapters in this book, we can benefit from looking at the reasons why a particular kind of conversation might be challenging. In the case of selling, it's clear to me that the very act of asking for the business feels needy, and that's all it takes for the conversation to be challenging. Add to that a pile of failed attempts at selling and we have a bad case on our hands. There is a very real heat in the vulnerability that comes from trying to sell, and failing. If you know it, you probably know it well.

The longer we go without a sale, the more difficult selling becomes. But there's hope.

How can we reframe how we look at selling, and, perhaps even anticipate a time when you'll have the confidence to pursue bigger pieces of business – the ones that make even old hands feel nervous again?

TELLING THE GREATER TRUTH ABOUT WHAT SELLING IS

It's really rather simple to reframe sales, which is a good thing, because that means you can start applying it right away, and make these conversations easier. Find a way to confess to your prospects that you would very much like to work with them. Get it out in the open, right at the outset, and the entire game changes.

You need something. (In this case, to sell something and presumably, bring money to your business.) The potential client needs something. (Possibly, they need what you have.) If these two things overlap, voila, the potential for a sale exists. If you hear echoes of Chapter Two, the Delta Model, here, you're perceptive, and getting the hang of it! This process is an elaboration of the questions 3 Delta questions we covered:

1. **Get clear on what you want.**

   This step asks 'Where are you now?' and 'Where do you want to go?' for you. And even though it seems very simple, it can take the breath away from some business owners, especially new ones, because you're so used to being told to sell something by being oblique or indirect. Eliminate the nerves and cut to the chase. You want something. Businesses exist to exchange something for money. Get clear about what you want in the sales conversation and readily confess it, no need to be sheepish.

2. Get clear on what the potential client wants.

This, on the other hand, is the 'Where are you now?' and 'Where would you like to go?' for the client, and where you get to listen. It's only when this step gets ignored that selling starts to feel manipulative. How many times have you said 'I really don't want this 3-pack of fancy chamois for my car" only to be ignored? That's because it's all about what the business owner wants – a sale. Selling is a relationship, and not listening to what the prospective client wants is just plain stupid.

Instead, I use a variation of this:

"Let me learn a little bit about you so that I can understand how I can help you. What is it that's most important to you right now?"

3. Find the overlap between #1 and #2.

In some cases, there may not be an overlap. Where you want to go and where the prospect wants to go have nothing in common. This is great because it's super clear. That's not a good client for you. No sale this time. Only when there IS overlap is there going to be the possibility for a sale.

And only if you don't reveal your agenda -- that you would like to make a sale, that you would like to acquire a client -- only THEN are you being manipulative, hoping the weird hope that somehow you can trick a person into buying something from you. Not only is it not truthful, it won't work.

You can't trick, or bore a person into being a long term, happy client. Note: you might succeed at doing it once. But tricking a person once and hoping they aren't too upset, isn't a good business strategy, especially if you want to grow, instead of sneak out of town.

OVER-ATTACHMENT LEADS TO HYPE, WHICH LEADS TO DISAPPOINTMENT

Selling conversations can become awkward and blow up in another instance -- when you're pushy in the extreme. Some of the outdated wisdom about selling encourages people to go for the sale at all costs, no matter what. This is a kind of Industrial Revolution-era thinking – there should be maximum effectiveness and potential from every interaction, therefore a business' sales process should be like a factory, and produce a bag of marshmallow icing every 3 seconds.

When we conduct sales from this perspective, getting over-attached, we can become sleazy or hype-y, saying anything to close the deal, losing our humanity. It's manipulative, and dis-honouring of both parties. If you're a caring human being, you will be committed, but not attached, in your selling process, and you'll accomplish that by listening.

Especially when times are tough, and you have a cash flow imperative, it can be difficult to stay unattached. So let's lay this out even more clearly:

Imagine you've talked to 10 people about what you have to sell. Each one of those people is going to fall into one of three categories:

> *Category #1: Yes, I want to buy*
>
> *Category #2: No, I am not interested*
>
> *Category #3: Maybe, I'll think about it.*

Where we start to feel the most manipulative and sleazy is when we try to force the 'maybe' pile into the 'yes' pile.

Instead, maybe we decide we're okay with backing off of the 'maybe' pile. Or, maybe we decide we want to be really thorough about it, and manage the 'maybes' in a follow up system so that the day they become a 'yes,' we'll know about it. Either works, and the job of deciding what kind of business person you'll be around the 'maybes' is yours to explore.

THE SAME APPLIES TO SELLING TO A GROUP

You're speaking to a group because you're interested in their business. No need to be coy. You ask what their goals are so you can see if you're equipped to help them. So far, so great. What else might happen when you're selling to a group?

1. **It's more complicated to listen to the needs of lots of people at once.**

   Suiting up, preparing your talk, and speaking to a group of people, you're ready. You've given talks in front of 10 people, and 100, maybe even 1,000. What happens when you invite them to purchase something for you?

   Unlike when you submit a proposal, or when you're on the phone with a potential buyer, you have more than one prospective client listening to your talk. What's just one way you can demonstrate you're listening well to the needs of so many individuals?

   Ask them to speak up.

"Raise your hand if you have any comments about the presentation so far. What's still unclear? What have you learned? What's changed since I started speaking?"

With the answers you get, you can demonstrate your listening chops by weaving their words into your invitation.

"Because like the gentleman in the third row, you may still feel unclear about how to go from here, I would like to invite you to consider joining us for our leadership retreat."

"The publicity campaign that I'll help you with will answer questions like the ones we've just heard."

Be as specific as you can in the moment.

2. Individuals in a group stop paying attention when they're bored.

Unlike an individual conversation, if you don't have a plan, you will lose the attention of a good number of your audience. An individual doesn't have a choice; if they start to daydream, it's noticeable. How do you ensure you keep the attention of as much of a group as possible?

There's no need to pretend you're a children's photographer, unless you are one of course, waving stuffed toys around and making funny noises. Instead, follow a simple set of guidelines for making a selling invitation to a group:

- Take the amount of time you have for your presentation, and find the 50-80% mark. If you have an hour, that'll be between 30-40 minutes.

- Pause the content of your presentation and interrupt yourself with an invitation. For best results, the invitation should have a close relationship with the content you're presentation. Example: If you're selling an apple pie recipe, you may be presenting on how to grow great apples.

- Clearly describe what you're selling, with the benefits highlighted by success stories your business can claim. Lay out the price point, and give clear directions on what to do, for those interested. Deliver this with the same upbeat energy that you delivered the first part of your content.

- After your invitation, return to your content and complete your presentation. In the final minutes of your time, remind the audience of your invitation and the specific action steps they can take to join you in your offering.

The process above gets much better with practice, and is worth spending time perfecting in your own way. The point is, we don't want you trying to ask for the business in the final minutes of your presentation time, when it's very easy to go overtime. Today's audiences are used to interruptions, and often pay more attention, not less, when you mix things up in an unorthodox way. Taking a bold stand for something you believe, and that your business stands for, in the content of your presentation will also work very well, by the way. But that's a topic for another day.

Starting with the points above, you'll keep the attention of a group audience, and thereby have the opportunity to interest them in what you're selling. Selling to a group is one of the most challenging things a business owner can learn to do. But that's probably the way it ought to be, since the rewards are potentially so good. You'd celebrate if you did a 60-minute talk to 100 people and 20 of them bought, right?

IF QUOTING OR SUBMITTING A PROPOSAL IS CHALLENGING, YOU'RE MISSING A STEP

Often, as a mentor to business owners, I hear the refrain, 'I have to submit a proposal for a 6-month project, and I have no idea what to quote. We talked for a long time, and the prospect seems quite excited, and now I have a deadline in two days, help!'

Here's what I'll say regarding this kind of selling process:

If you don't know what to quote, you don't have enough information.

It's that simple. Quoting on a big piece of business should never be a shot in the dark. It's not in the best interest of the prospect, either, so the experienced ones may give you a hand and say, 'We have a budget of (insert range) so I'd like your proposal to come in there somewhere.'

More often than not though, this kind of prospect has a lot going on, so if you don't ask them for their budget, they may forget, or, simply not think to tell you. After all, it's your job to show them you know your stuff. Here's some language for you to try on:

"Thanks for all of that information. It gives me an excellent idea of what you're looking for, and I'm confident we can help."

"Do you have some thoughts about the budget you'd like to stay within for this work?"

"It's already the last quarter of the year, and I'm not sure how you like to do your budgeting. When are you wanting this work to happen and what kind of budget have you set previously?"

"There are a lot of ways we can do this, including the luxury version and the budget version, what would you say you're looking for?"

Are you wanting me to quote you for the entire project at once, or would it help to break it down into phases? (If the answer is phases, keep asking! What kind of phases and what budget for each?)

It sounds like you're thinking of having a large number of people take part. Do you usually like to be quoted per person, by retainer, or in another way?

I'd love to hear more about your preferences for quoting so I can get as close to the mark as possible in my proposal.

If I can deliver all the things you want, with flying colours, what is your budget?

The leverage you use in getting this information is simple. It lives in the overlap in your goals – to get a great proposal together efficiently and get going with the work. So don't hesitate to use these points:

"We're all very busy, and I respect your time, so could you tell me as much as you can about what dollar amounts will work for you? This will save me from troubling you with another call later."

"This sounds very exciting. I'd love to make sure we're in the same ballpark regarding fees, so I can save you from reviewing a proposal that just doesn't work."

"I'm sure you're eager to get this work done so you can move onto other challenges, would you help me understand what would be an easy yes when it comes to fees for this work? I'd hate to get us bogged down when summer is so close and your busy season around the corner."

"Our company is a boutique, and we'd be honored to have you as a client. My partner told me this morning that we may be looking at a later start for new client work after this month, so in the interest of expediting this, what's a number I can use for fees when I go to design the program?"

The same thing goes for anything else you need to know when putting together a proposal. There are two consistent stuck points and one variable:

One (1) the fees, and two (2) when the prospect wants to get started. Be sure to apply the same line of questioning about timeframes while you're in the trenches about the budget.

The variable stuck point has to do with the objections that come up in the process after the proposal has been sent, such as 'I like this other company's proposal better' or 'I heard from a former client of yours who didn't like you' and a myriad other things, which is more than what we can cover here. Suffice to say that none of these is insurmountable, and you can get started detangling these by reviewing Chapters Two and Three.

And there you have it. How to ask for the bigger sale, and a whole passel of language you can use to alleviate the challenges that come up, including several common selling scenarios.

"Whatever you do, be different – that was the advice my mother gave me, and I can't think of better advice for an entrepreneur. If you're different, you will stand out."

ANITA RODDICK

CHAPTER 10

Inspiring Breakthrough Performance

Some of the most important business conversations you'll ever have are the ones you have with yourself.

While writing this book, I spent a good chunk of time at an Outdoor Education Centre called Strathcona Park Lodge. Besides being a terrific lake retreat for writing, I was so impressed by their 'Code of Ethics/Fact Check,' which included, among other things: Challenge at the edge/Choose own edge. As one of their values.

One of the rewards of being in business is the ability to create this kind of experience for ourselves, and the teams we lead.

When you talk to yourself about your business, what would happen if, instead of accepting the status quo, you asked yourself what it might take to inspire exceptional performance in your business at every juncture? In a very real sense, you're perhaps more than a little like God, creating something out of nothing, and you have the chance to be more than ordinary. Strathcona Park Lodge doesn't need to have a 'Code of Ethics' but they do. They seek to navigate the extra challenge because they can.

Creating a culture of excellence involves vision, guts and time. You may have those ingredients, or, you may need to be patient and allow them to accumulate. Meanwhile, what everyone can do, starting right away, is interact with people in your sphere on a more granular basis with this in mind. Whether it be in performance reviews, hiring conversations, work with your clients, or, plain old reflection of your own about the future, these add up. Over time, you'll have a culture built in an organic way.

Here are some coaching tools for generating breakthroughs, one conversation at a time.

COACHING TOOL #1: TRANSFERRING EXCELLENCE

Because not everyone is looking to achieve excellence every day, it can be prudent to start gently. One of the most enjoyable ways is to look for excellence somewhere else in the person's life. Maybe they are an amazing chef, or soccer player, or always dress stylishly. You may have a former Olympian, Chess Champion or die-hard macramé artist as one of your consultants.

Whatever the area of excellence is, the flow state and muscle memory this person has built into their life can be plugged into, and transferred to other areas of their life. All you need do is invite them to try it. It also works well to help someone with an area they're struggling in.

> "I know there's a lot of paperwork that needs sorting right now and it can be really overwhelming. I was hoping that we could find a way to inject some energy into it and get it done. I happened to remember that you love to make jewelry, haven't you been doing that for quite a few years?"

> "Yeah, I've won a couple of awards over the years, and sometimes I get commissions from stores for those pieces, which is fun."

> "That's so impressive. I can barely choose jewelry that looks good on me! You know, it occurs to me - when

you're making jewelry with all those parts and such, beads, wire, tools, little tiny pieces of things, is it ever overwhelming? How do you handle that?"

"Well, yes it can be, but it helps to sort things into piles, so it's not all a jumble, and that simplifies things a lot. And if I have a really big piece, or I'm trying to make a lot of things at once, I chunk the job down instead of working on the whole big thing. And then of course, keeping in mind the finished project, and how great that will feel when it's complete always gives me energy."

"That is really neat. You've obviously found a way to excel there and I can tell you love it! I know it's really different, but, maybe in some ways it's similar... with the paperwork in the office, is it possible to look at it in the same way as when you have a whole bunch of busy work for a jewelry project? Are there similarities do you think?"

"I guess there is. I feel kind of stuck because I don't know how to sort the paperwork, it just feels like one big blur. I guess if I could figure out some buckets then I could chunk things down. Kind of like I have a way to sort different colour beads."

"How about if you tried that and then run it by me, and I can help? I'm thinking that once all that paper is

sorted it's going to feel amazing, and a big weight off of everyone."

"Sure. I guess I can see that it's a lot like cleaning up after a big jewelry workshop. It's a one-time job, and if we're organized about the cleanup, the next cleanup will be easier. So I could look at it like that."

"That's great. I know it's not as much fun as jewelry-making maybe, but, each piece of paper is a little like a bead, in a way. I'd love to have that job done, when do you think is a good deadline for it… you know, like a client who's waiting for her necklace?"

"Oh, sure. How about Monday? That gives me three days this week. If I need more time I should know pretty quick. I can let you know."

Of course, sometimes getting a person to do their job wants to be much more straightforward than this. You may not have the luxury of time to try it, and if you do, not everyone will respond positively. Also, sometimes the comparison doesn't work!

But I've come to trust the transferring excellence exercise – if I show a sincere interest in the person's area of awesomeness, it allows that version of the person to show up. Helping them see they can be that person as they do the job I need them to do, works, even if only energetically.

Where can you apply the idea of transferring excellence in your business? You might think twice and consider yourself. Whatever's on your 'Ugh' list, what thing is it a little bit 'like?' Choose something you love and start making connections. You might find a surprising way to uplevel those 'Ughs' and make them 'Oooh ahhhhhs.'

COACHING TOOL #2: THE TAKE-AWAY MANEUVER

Let's say you have someone in front of you who really wants something, but they're having difficulty achieving it and a lot of time is passing. Even though it's got them stuck, they lust madly after this goal. Maybe you're a consultant, and your client wants to win a prestigious industry award. Or, you're a coach of some kind, and your client wants to write a book, rebrand their website, get into their favourite dress, or work up the courage to propose marriage to the person you helped them meet.

Within your business, you might have someone who has a pet project that they're in charge of in addition to their regular work. Say your office manager has a budget to paint and redecorate the lobby. This is something they'd love to do, and do really well, but they're getting tangled in the weeds and have been stuck for a good amount of time. It's all talk, no action.

What can you the business owner do to help in situations like these? Move things along because there are other priorities that need attention and time's a'wasting.

Try seeing it like this:

When any kind of significant action is being contemplated like in the scenarios above, it's a little like standing at the edge of a cliff. With toes lined up at the edge, the person is in the right spot to jump across the 'gap' and get to the other side. Except, in this case, there's inertia. No movement, and seemingly, no way to generate movement. What to do?

What can you do to give a person momentum when they're standing still? The answer is to take something away. In essence you're removing the edge of the cliff they're standing on, so they have no choice but to move – quick!

For the person who wants to write a book, but just isn't:

"Angie, I think you should just give up on the idea of a book. It's been four months since we started the project and we're still going in circles. I think you actually don't want to do it, so it would just be healthier to say that and cross that off. Move on to other dreams."

For the Office Manager:

"So Natalie, I know you were excited about the redecoration project for the lobby, but it's been almost a year and it's

not done yet. What do you say we cancel it and just leave it? Or we can get Jerry to do it."

For the Coaching Client:

"Brian, you've been talking about proposing to Myrna for a long time. I know you're still working on your feelings of rejection from your previous marriage. I want you to feel 100% sure about this, so I say, back down from this for now. If you're not a hell yes now, maybe you're just meant to be in a relationship and not bother with making it official. How about we call it 'good' and stop pursuing marriage?"

Too often with long-held goals, human beings get complacent. Their goal becomes their teddy bear, and achieving the goal actually triggers the anxiety of the familiar teddy bear going away.

The Take-Away Maneuver removes the comfort level of the status quo, taking away the 'cliff' underneath their toes. Even though the actual person hasn't moved, movement has been created.

There are some typical responses to using this coaching tool:

"Yeah, you're right. I guess I just don't want to write the book enough to get going. It's a nice dream, but I agree.

Crossing it off feels like a relief, and actually makes me realize it's been burdening me. Maybe I can get some other stuff done instead of worrying about the book I'm not writing!"

"No way, Jerry is going to do a terrible job of redecorating. You can't take this project away from me. I've just been stuck on what shade of green for the paint! I know it doesn't matter really, I've just been procrastinating. I'll decide today and I can get the painters in next week!"

"Gosh, I dunno. Marriage means a lot to Myrna, but you're right, I'm still just one foot in the door, one foot out. I'm tired of that. I don't think I want to rule marriage out, but I definitely need to do something different to get past my fears. What do you think of doing some focused work on those fears, or, maybe speaking to Myrna directly about them? I thought proposing to her should be a surprise, but, at the rate I'm going I'm never going to get to it, so just spitting it out to her that I've been considering it could be good."

There may be acceptance of your take-away, giving up on the goal and releasing energy for the future. There may be pent-up 'No way!' energy and rapid, decisive movement towards the goal. Or there may be acknowledgement that something needs to change. Whatever the result, using the take-away to change a stuck status quo is really delightful.

WE NEED TO TALK Andrea J. Lee

I think you'll find it very rewarding, even if you just start with yourself.

COACHING TOOL #3: SIZE OF CANVAS

From time to time you'll come across a situation where something is stuck in such a way that confounds you despite the best advice you get. A previously high-performing team member has lost it and is unrecognizable. An important project is grinding to a halt, and the engine overheated. What the heck is going on here?

The reasons can be many, but one effective way to change things up is to consider the size of canvas, and the size of the paintbrush you're metaphorically employing. Here's an example:

You're hosting a 3-day workshop and it is more significant, in every way, than anything you've done before. Expectations for the number of attendees is at least 5 times more than your biggest workshop in the past. You're setting a new bar for production values so décor, design, client care, and content being taught must be impeccable. The experience needs to be commensurate with the ticket price attendees are paying – you're aiming for a 'wow' that leads to substantial new and repeat business for the next 2 years.

With a thousand details on hand, you're instinct to delegate is probably immediate, and that's great. But it's still all moving far too slowly and something is just not sitting up straight and coming together the way it needs to.

Instead of thinking about the entire event as one giant canvas, the size of the side of a house, and you're trying to create that, try breaking it down into smaller pieces.

In the course of three days you'll have three mornings and three afternoons, each of which has two chunks of time in it, before and after the break. That's a total of 12 pieces. Much like large art installations that utilize 12 small canvases to make up a single larger visual image, consider how you might work on (and complete) the 12 separate canvases of your workshop.

Chunk #1 is your introduction and set up. Not a whole lot of pressure there, it's a more functional piece of time that sets the tone of things. Same for Chunk #2, it's the conclusion of your entire event. Recaps, takeaways, exhortations for what to do after going home, you can handle this chunk easily too. Mentally check these off and you now have 10 smaller chunks. Much easier to go one by one and sort these out than trying to paint the larger canvas all at once.

Size of a Paintbrush

The notion of the size of paintbrush can also be useful. Think of it this way -- if you're trying to paint the giant canvas with the tiny brush inside a watercolor kit, you may as well quit now, both for your sake and the brush's!

In what way have you been holding your energy like a tiny brush, trying to paint a huge canvas?

High achievers tend to do this, and mentally shifting your thinking construct to right-size both canvas and brush are excellent methods to change how you accomplish things.

What's an example of a size of brush adjustment for our workshop example? If someone is obsessing about the precise shade of the colour in the logo on the presentation slides, that's a size of brush issue. Whether or not the nametags should say the name of city and country, or just city, is another example. These fine-brush details are just fine to address, but not as a priority. They are the weeds we get stuck in at the expense of broad and medium-brush questions like 'Of the 10 chunks of time I have to deliver content, what will be the three main points in each section?' Or 'How can I get the best results from the invitation I'll make to attendees that will attract them to work with my business after the workshop?' Once the right big and medium brush questions are addressed, often the tiny brush actions will have taken care of themselves.

If not though, it's fine to leave them.

Artists who paint on large canvases will tell you. Start with the broad brush strokes in the major colours you want for your finished product. Only once that's done do the small brushes come out.

Sit down and take stock now. What challenges are you grappling with that have to do with you using a tiny paintbrush to fill a huge canvas? Is exhaustion part of it? Use the proper tool for the job and you'll have your breakthrough.

COACHING TOOL #4: BREADCRUMBS OF SUCCESS

Often the big breakthroughs cause people to freeze up and paralyze -- because we're asking their brain and their soul and their heart to all go forward together and create this huge breakthrough. The person is maybe still developing to the place where they can hold a big breakthrough like that. Instead, pull back and just ask, where is the joy?

Getting Permission to Give Tough Love

The opportunities available to any given business to produce breakthrough results are countless. They're all around you, like the air your breathe. The world around us conspires to rob us of our power, and we can be on the edge of giving up on a lot of things. You may feel like you and others around you have been brainwashed in some way and you're just waking up as you read this book and pursue your version of unplugging from the Borg that controlled your thoughts.

It's not you. It's the Industrial Revolution values that our world has been formed by for well over 100 years. We're accustomed to looking for a map and believing that that map is 'it' and we stop thinking.

But when you're part of an entrepreneurial endeavor, you're very much a part of a rebellion to take back our minds and think for ourselves.

When it comes to waking others up around you, be aware that you're pulling back the blinders and revealing a kind of truth. Sometimes this can go badly, with people preferring the old way. Hey, we all have days like that!

It's best to ask permission. In whatever way that you can find to ask permission, and get buy-in from the person you're talking to, do it. Just because you see that the person in front of you could have a breakthrough, doesn't mean you should always go for it.

"On a scale of 1 to 10, I can tell you the extreme version of what I see or I can tell you the mini version of what I see. Which would you prefer? What number would you prefer?"

"On a scale of 1 to 10 I feel like there are degrees of this learning that I could share with you and I just want to respect that you might not be ready for the full 10 today. So you pick a number and tell me to what degree you'd like for me to go for it."

"So I think that there are several lessons here that are available. Which lesson would you like to learn?"

"Would you like to learn the deepest lesson or would you like to learn a more short-term lesson?"

"The choice here for me in this moment would be to give you a short-term answer to your question or I can also give you a long-term answer to your question. Would you like a short-term answer only or would you like for me to give you the short-term answer and the long-term answer?"

"What is essential is invisible to the eye."

LE PETIT PRINCE, ANTOINE DE ST. EXUPÉRY

CHAPTER 11

Income Generation When Nothing Seems to Work

When cash flow is at a low point and stress is high, the conversations we have with ourselves become even more crucial. Because at those times, and in times of rapid change, ordinary income stream generation isn't going to work. We need to be honest with ourselves in order to uncover our fastest path to cash.

WHAT IS CASH?

Cash is a representation of value. It's like when you go to a restaurant and you look at a menu and the menu is the representation of the food. You can't eat the menu, but it is an ambassador of the food. Cash is an ambassador or a representation of something else and its value.

So now…what is value?

Value happens when human beings want something and get it. Value is being exchanged. If somebody doesn't want anything, if nobody wants anything, then no value can be exchanged.

There are things that we are selling and buying right now that we had no idea we would be buying and selling right now 10 years ago. Value shifts with society's desires. We need to be talking about what our value is much more than we might think. If we don't help to create a market for our newer thing, people are not going to come to us to exchange cash with us in the amounts that we want. Because our stuff is new we have to create the market demand as well as the supply. We're not just the supply side; we have to work on the demand side. If there's no demand, we don't need to supply.

One of those things we can sometimes forget as entrepreneurs is that what we're actually doing is educating people as to our value. If people don't understand that there's value here, then cash can't happen, especially if you're doing a new thing.

How can we help ourselves and our clients create more cash?

Knowledge

Being an entrepreneur, you have an essential need for a certain kind of knowledge. No coach is going to be worth their salt if they don't continuously expand their actual knowledge. This is facts and figures, understanding of the market, conceptual things – just the smarts of how to make money.

There are three basic ways that any business can make money.

According to Jay Abraham, they are:

a. Raise the price on whatever it is you're currently offering.

b. Increase the number of units you sell.

c. Sell more things to the same customer.

This will help you make decisions about where you want to focus your efforts in order to make more cash.

A key area of knowledge is ways we can add value. There are a lot of ways that businesses like ours can do that, and there is big money to be made – including money to be made that other people are not yet understanding. The reality is, human beings are evolving and our needs and desires are changing. That means value is changing too.

Value is understood only within the context of what's important to a society. And if what's important to a society is changing, then our value is going to change too, and our skills to communicate this new value must keep up.

So what are some other ways we can add value?

- Expertise
- Get stuff done for people
- Experience
- Relationships or who you know
- Communication or how you make meaning
- Persuasion or the influence that you can have
- Leadership
- Attention and time you have to spend focusing on something. (Attention is one of the values that I think is underrated, especially for beginner entrepreneurs. As a new business coach you might have more time that you could spend focusing on a client and that would provide more value to the client.)
- Pleasure and the enjoyment you bring
- Accountability or how things get done
- Status or credibility that you've earned.

For example, it used to be that people would pay a lot of money to hurry up. We would pay to get on a plane; we would pay to get something done faster – more, more, more and faster, faster, faster. But the context of doing business has changed. People are valuing things other than speed now.

If you'd like to make money, you need to add more value. If something you used to sell and sell well isn't selling well anymore, the value for that thing has diminished over time.

You need to find a new way to add value or your business and income streams will be in trouble.

Imagine someone comes up to you and they have their thing that they brought to the swap meet and you look at each other and you look at your thing and on an intuitive level you don't want to trade. There's not enough value in the exchange.

If we can't feel the value in that thing that that person has, then we're not going to give up our thing.

What does this mean for your business? If we have trouble selling, could it be because they don't see the value in it? So then what is your job? Add more value to it and then communicate with your buyers to educate the value of it.

The emotion that we want to have happen in our businesses: that both sides of the equation, the person who's selling and the person who's receiving, are thrilled, over the moon, like the other person got ripped off! We want our businesses to thrive on this emotional resonance of we're giving so much value that the customer is thrilled to trade their dollars, to come type in their credit card numbers for it.

If you can hold onto this excitement about exchanging value and hang on to this concept about creating a business where your customers are willingly and happily parting with their cash for your things, you're going to be way advanced.

Exercises.

Exercises are often underrated as a tool through which to achieve breakthroughs and create results.

Some exercises I particularly love include:

a. Case studies.

Offer your thing for free, or at least for a very low price, so that you can prove your amazingness. If we have a new idea, it's very difficult to convey the value of it from a stand still.

Going out and coaching 100 people for free, and understanding and proving, and creating case studies is a very real way of helping you build a foundation towards cash.

Then once you've done your case study, the second step is to transfer the case studies over into an actual offer. How do you do that? The key points are this: you need to gain testimonials, you need to show that you've made a delta (there's that word again!) or you've made a change in the client's results.

b. The peanut butter cup.

Think of your current business as either peanut butter or chocolate. If you can find the other element and add it to your business, the shazam moment becomes possible. When this amazing, fresh combination arrives in the market, nobody else can touch it. It's a market innovation that touches on a new desire and offers the supply of something that's valuable.

And you are in a category of one, because you've created something so fresh.

c. The oyster grit

When we are having conversations around how to create more cash, one of the best ways to land on new income streams, to spice up old income streams, sell more units and also sometimes raise the price is to ask yourself this question"

"What is the one thing that really bugs me in the area where I'm providing my product or service?

It's like the grit in the oyster that just drives you batty -- and if you allow yourself to feel into this emotional resonance, as an entrepreneur that's not just a pearl; it's a whole bag of pearls.

Authority and the edge.

When you communicate with people in business, there are times when it's important for them to know that you mean business. Especially with coaching clients. Think of a dog: when you speak to a dog with authority and the edge, he responds.

Here are some great questions to ask that will show authority and the edge with a client that is making a commitment:

"What would happen if you don't follow through on this?"
"What would happen if you do follow through?"
"How important is it to you that you do this?"
"And what's the cost to you if you don't do this?"

Those are questions that raise the stakes on the edge, which can help you use your potential client's motivation.

Once that's been established, your next step is to set a time frame, and then follow-up.

ONE FINAL POINT ON CREATING CASH...

As soon as a person has made their first dollar, creating more cash is all about repeating what works. What worked the very best in the entire history of your business? Figure out what has worked the best and repeat it.

And finally, here are a few conversations to have with yourself when you need to create cash.

Think of a beloved project or income stream that didn't sell. How can I add more value to my offering? How can I communicate that value to the perfect people?

1. Choose one of the exercises (case studies, peanut butter cup, and oyster grit).

2. How could I create a new income stream, so I can sell more to my existing clients, using one of these exercises?

Think of a time a client did not get the result they were hoping for when they signed up to work with me. How could I use the authority and the edge to help the client achieve more?

What has worked for me in the past in terms of creating cash? What is my plan to repeat what worked?

*"War is for the weak.
Peace is for the strong."*

STELLA GHERVAIS

CHAPTER 12

Assuming Stronger Leadership

As you absorb this book, you may find yourself fatigued. Working inside businesses is not a walk in the park, and gone are the days of plum paychecks, long lunches and security. So if a small part of you is resisting the reality of the conversations ahead of you, take heart. This chapter is about supporting you in the pursuit of what's sacred to you, why you cared enough in the first place to do what you do. In short, it's about strengthening what's holy in you.

You would be right if you're gathering that one of the bigger themes of this book is each of us assuming greater leadership. It's as if the world is climbing Mt. Everest and there is a shortage of guides. It's a journey that is fraught, but boy is the summit worthwhile. Anyone who feels the smallest ping to help make the ascent is saying yes to becoming a stronger leader. Everyone who does that immediately commands every inch of my support, and my highest regard.

So let's see if we can remind ourselves a little bit of why we're here in the first place, shall we? Why would you want to assume more leadership, to lead cool things?

In my opinion, you're leading one of the coolest things that exist on the planet -- and that is a thing called a small business, or the equivalent. A business in which you get to decide exactly what you do every day. You get to decide what difference you want to make in the lives of your clients. You get to decide that when Martians arrive on earth and they look at you as a business owner and as a human being, they conclude, making a note on their clipboards, that you did something great.

But to help us find the energy to sustain us, I find it pays to remember the stakes.

When we're leading cool things it's natural to have some fear, because we may not have been groomed to lead cool things. Are you doing just fine, as is, do you have to go to that 'next level?' It can be natural to shrink a little bit in the face of cool things and being the leader. But if cool things are finding you, you can bet that it means something. Cool things don't land at just anyone's feet. And leadership is not for the faint of heart.

There are three stories I want to leave with you that I think really serve the purpose of raising the stakes. They are the stories that nourish me when times are hard. They help me remember why I try to do good, and right, especially when things are challenging. When appropriate, I use them shamelessly to remind others. The first is about a man named Cortez.

CORTEZ AND THE COMMAND TO 'BURN THE SHIPS!'

Cortez was an explorer who had landed on a certain piece of land, unknown, and not their intended destination, at least probably not. It had been an arduous journey and the way forward was terribly uncertain.

Upon coming ashore, it became clear that the sailors and the people on his ship were unhappy. They threatened to mutiny. They wanted to go back to their homes, many leagues away, and forgo the journey to discover the secret treasure that was rumored to be somewhere in the region.

WE NEED TO TALK Andrea J. Lee

Maybe it wasn't really there anyway.

Assessing the situation, Cortez did something that he's become famous for. He had all the ships burned to the ground. And in doing so, he cut off all ties he and his crew had to their homes. He made it impossible to look back.

Faced with no other option but forward, this group of explorers made homes in the region where they landed on, which in years to come, would be known as Veracruz.

The second story takes place in a more modern setting, in a casino. And since we're using our imaginations, why don't we make it a super posh casino, one that, say, James Bond might be seen in? You're in your dressed-up best, with a wad of cash, ready to pick a table and play. Mmm. Yes, that'll do the trick nicely.

WHAT WOULD IT TAKE TO PUSH ALL YOUR CHIPS IN?

Picture yourself sitting at a table -- you're gambling. It doesn't matter what game it is, but this isn't a garage full of friends, or a neighbourhood mahjong game with grandma. We're talking about some high-rollers.

As you watch the film, notice yourself in this setting. Are you at ease? Is the $100 martini, extra olives, amusing or outrageous to you? At the table, are you betting one chip at a time, playing carefully and looking to make incremental gains? Confidence builds over time, do you continue with your strategy or try a bigger move? Interesting.

When you're leading cool things as an entrepreneur, there is plenty at stake, in business and in life. Money is a given. But there's also your reputation, the trust people have in you that could be jeopardized, and the cause – the thing you hope will be better because of your business.

In the life cycle of a business, there are moments when betting one chip at a time is just not going to cut it. Making a plan to leap from six figures to seven, for example. You can't sell just a little bit more of what you already have. The prize is not reachable that way. Nope. Bolder moves are required.

What would it take, back inside our film at the casino, for you to look at the reality of the game, take some deep breaths, wiggle your toes, and push your entire stack of chips into the middle of the table?

What move are you contemplating that would require you to let go of your current safe reality and move those chips? Maybe it's inside your business, but sometimes this exercise brings up dreams for brand new businesses. Outrageous ideas. Thoughts of throwing it all in.

With that in mind, one chip at a time, is that going to do it, do you think?

The energy of being 'all-in' is unencumbered and bracing unlike any other, and is the hallmark of being a leader. While others are content, you have ideas that will not release you. Visualizing yourself in the gambling scene can be great mental preparation ahead of doing it in real life.

The final story I use to motivate myself when I'm preparing for a leap is fairly ironic, because I haven't played many sports, and definitely haven't had the experience of playing on a team like soccer or hockey. Still, I've built teams throughout my entrepreneurial career, so I have a very real sense of what it feels like.

If you've played team sports though, this will be useful. Call up some of your favourite memories from that time in your life. And even if you haven't, like me, this will still work. Just lean on whatever you can access around team sports – maybe it's from watching them on television, or, having family members who play.

ARE YOU PLAYING OFFENSE, OR DEFENSE?

So we're looking at a soccer game, and notice that something is very wrong. The teams are on the field, but there is very little action. It becomes clear what's happening. The score is zero, and the players are protecting their net. They're playing defensively, and no one is trying to score a goal.

Think about it for a moment. If no one plays offense, what is the highest score possible in this game?

If you answered zero, you're right.

In your business and life, are there ways in which you're playing just defense, and protecting yourself? Are you forgetting that to put a score on the board, you have to go out and play some offense? Protecting your goal might be alright if you're already ahead, but in times of change, staying in the same spot means you're falling behind. Protecting yourself isn't going to allow you to survive.

In a lot of ways, when faced with leadership challenges, we find ourselves shrinking, retracting, protecting ourselves. It's natural. In the school of hard knocks, who wouldn't take a moment to gather themselves before deciding to play full out? When I'm challenging myself to assume greater leadership and do what only I'm able to do, fulfilling my purpose as a business leader, I ask myself:

Am I playing to win, or am I playing not to lose?

How long will I play defense, before I get out there and take an offensive shot on the goal of life?

What will it take for me to go out there and be offensive?

ARE THEY WITH YOU? GALVANIZING YOUR TEAM

It's one thing to have a bold vision and be ready to burn the ships, put all your chips in the middle of the table and play to win. That's a lot! What's even better is if you can find a talented team that wants to go with you, and is so on fire, they own the vision with you.

In the beginning, it can take some time to sort out how to do this. Begin with three simple explorations:

1. Find out what motivates them not just in their role with you but in their life. What pushes their happy buttons?

2. Share your vision for the project or business. Speak candidly about why you're impassioned by it and what you hope the business can contribute to the bigger world.

3. Examine whether there is an overlap between #1 and #2.

An excellent example of this is my partnership with Indrani Goradia, Founder of the Indrani's Light Foundation, a not-for-profit organization that we run very much like a business – which is a powerful trend in the world of philanthropy. This is what Indrani says:

"I want to end gender based violence in the world within my lifetime. I want my grandchildren to say 'Gender

violence, what is that?' and have to go to Google to find out what it is."

And this is what I have to say about my life and work:

"I'd like for the world to know that until we work with not just the victims of violence, but with the perpetrators, who are also victims, we cannot solve the problem of Gender-Based Violence. New victims of GBV are the new perpetrators waiting to happen. I want us to work together, beyond the labels, to bring about peace."

You can deduce the overlap between these two things. It's powerful, and the teamwork that's emerged between Indrani and me as a result is greater than what either one of us could do alone. Though not every overlap will have the strength of a gale-force wind like this, this is the kind of activated, pulling-together team you can commit to building too.

It's worth it. You just need to talk about it.

A NEW ERA FOR LEADERSHIP

This is a tough topic worth touching on at least a little. Traditional leadership structures are rapidly giving way to more innovative ways to build businesses. Thankfully, there is a new model in town and it looks like this:

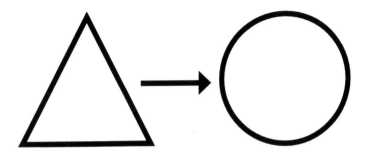

The Old Paradigm

Leadership these days looks very different from the kind we got used to in the post-Industrial Revolution era. It was really bureaucratic. There was someone at the top of the triangle and everybody else fell in underneath. It was hierarchical. Perhaps your business is run like this, because it's what you've known.

The New Paradigm

Although relatively new, and therefore less proven, new businesses with younger leaders are demonstrating they can lead in circle formation instead of triangle. This means that although there's still a leader, the job of the leader is to facilitate the team. Instead of telling, we ask, then come to consensus. Instead of always knowing the answers, we defer to smarter people on the team to know better and take turns leading. Instead of laboring in secret for months before releasing a product to the market, we beta test with the market, making clients our partners, and create offerings that are shaped by real desires from real people. It's much less hierarchical, more resilient, and more failsafe -- but it does take time to do it this way.

Experimental and exciting, expect to hear more about this paradigm of leadership and how by adopting it, many of the more classical 'business challenges' and 'difficult conversations' simply don't even happen.

Just one last thing on the topic of saying yes to your leadership…

I once read an article in the Wall Street Journal called 'Why Doctors Die Differently.' In it, it was revealed that the vast majority of doctors would not opt for heroic measures to save them at the end of their lives. Those electric paddles that jump start your heart? They wouldn't want those, or any number of other last-minute efforts.

In addition to influencing me when it comes to my end of life wishes, this article gave me this clarity:

> *"I do not want to have heroic measures at the end of my life. I want to have heroic measures during my life."*

If there is a time to go for it, nothing held back, it's now, not later, at the last minute. I'd like to have those heroic

WE NEED TO TALK   Andrea J. Lee

measures now. As for the end of my life? I've decided I'm with the doctors. I'm not interested in heroic measures at the end, so long as I've employed them until that point.

To be clear…heroically doesn't mean working really hard and putting yourself in the grave early, either. It can mean heroically sitting in your hammock and heroically taking vacation when it's perfect. Because vacation-taking is heroic.

So think about this as you consider what leadership move you might be willing to take next, how you'll play full out with whatever move you're making. Whether you're ready sooner rather than later to make that secret dream come true. And consider whether your most challenging business conversations take on a new hue.

*"If you're brave enough to say goodbye,
life will reward you with a new hello."*

PAUL COELHO

CHAPTER 13
Graceful Goodbyes

As any child who ever owned a pet knows, goodbyes are an unavoidable part of life. This is especially true in business, where firings, resignations, stepping-down and even sometimes giving up are a part of the landscape. And while some goodbyes may be difficult, talking about them – both with the person departing and with ourselves – can make the difference between a graceful goodbye and an ugly goodbye.

Here are some techniques I like to use in the area of goodbyes.

SEEING WHAT CLIENTS DON'T SEE

One of the ways that I know I add great value to my clients is in the fact that as entrepreneurs, I know they are going to be hiring and firing team members, people on their leadership team, vendors -- even clients, if you want to look at it that way.   But because most entrepreneurs are focused on creating income and serving and that kind of thing, usually they don't think too far ahead as far as hiring and firing.

But even beyond that, it's not occurring to them just yet that looking into the future, they're actually going to be hiring and firing versions of themselves. And that's true for you reading this book, too. There's going to be a moment in time when you are going to fire the version of yourself that is holding you back -- for example, from earning what you're worth.

But if you're like most business owners, you're so focused on making this month's rent and paying the bills that you're not seeing in between the lines; you're not seeing what's coming next.

What I do is, I anticipate those goodbyes for my clients. And I make it my goal to give them a strong ending. I noticing and observing ahead of time, before the client themselves, that they are getting close to being done. Simply communicating that to the client is often a real catalyst for the work to take on an even sweeter taste.

GOING DEEP

Learning to get out of your head and drop into your heart is a key skill. This is another area where the Delta Model can help you go deeper.

Think of your favorite meal.

Now think of the first bite. Can you feel the salivary glands start to activate? And now skip ahead and think of the last couple of bites.

There's something special about the quality of those last couple of bites.

So much magic happens at the edges, in the goodbyes.

Your conversation might sound like this:

Where are you now?

> *"Well, I'm feeling a little frustrated. I wish I could get somewhere faster with my business. I'm scared quite honestly and I don't know what to do."*

Where would you like to go?

"I'd love to be proud of my business. I'd love to be confident and filled with self-respect for achieving something, and joyful."

The question is, how do you get from one emotional state to the other?

When I wake up in the morning and face my customers, clients, my most-favorite partners, my incredible team, my leadership team, I know that there's going to be day when we part ways and we say goodbye. And my heart opens in that goodbye because I know that it helps me enjoy today.

There's an interesting band of activity that starts and stops where things end and begin.

In the middle, our awareness is different; it's the same for relationships and building businesses.

As an entrepreneur, you are going to have goodbyes and hellos on two significant levels: Income and relationships.

SOME EXAMPLES OF GOODBYES

<u>Income</u>

- income level
- tax bracket
- streams of income
- debt

<u>Relationships</u>

- clients
- teams and team members
- joint venture relationships or partners
- vendors

SOME FINAL THOUGHTS ON GOODBYES

How might you communicate to clients that you have looked ahead and see the natural goodbye that is coming? How would that feel if that was on the receiving end of that greater truth?

What relationships, with yourself or outside of yourself, is it time to say goodbye to?

What sources or levels of income is it time to say goodbye to? What could you do to go deeper into that conversation with yourself to say goodbye? What are you saying hello to, in turn?

Living the Questions

"Opportunities don't knock, they whisper. So shut up, and listen."

THOMAS LEONARD

CHAPTER 14

Getting Your Needs Met

A Guest Chapter by Thomas Leonard

This chapter was written by my mentor, Thomas Leonard, long before I ever had the idea to write this book. Upon reading it, I think you'll agree that he still has a lot to contribute on the topic of how we talk to ourselves and get our very unique set of needs met as entrepreneurs.

NOTE: Entrepreneurs are jugglers by nature. Short of gene therapy, we are not going to change...

TIP: Come to understand yourself as an entrepreneur...

It's likely that you operate with a different set of rules that most people.

Dynamic: Your push/pull relationship with 'focus.'

Entrepreneurs KNOW they should focus vs. juggle. For many entrepreneurs, the word 'focus' is synonymous with the words prison, trapped, limited, boring and end-of-life-as-I-know-it. Checklists, management, and people development are generally not that appealing to entrepreneurs. We usually have to outsource these to others, to key staff, or to other firms to handle.

Entrepreneurs usually need more support than direction.

Entrepreneurs are like kings and queens of their kingdoms. We know how they want to run things. Everyone else is one of the subjects. (I am exaggerating, for effect.) What they usually want is about 80% support/encouragement/agreement and about 20% direction. Don't be surprised if you look for direction, but realize you don't want any!

Instead, you really crave feeling heard/supported. Get this need met and you'll begin to feel a lot better, fast.

Also, entrepreneurs like to be stimulated.

We crave stimulation. So, whether it's a question that captures our attention, a comment/observation someone makes about our business/idea, or a big, big request, think big. Entrepreneurs love the challenge. Too small or too niggling and you'll become bored.

As entrepreneurs, we want/need to be listened to. A lot.

The entrepreneur most needs to be heard. We want our ideas to be heard, our stresses, our good/great news, our special-ness. It's a craving; it's a need; it's just part of the dynamic of being an entrepreneur. (You might want to notice that it is likely your spouse is very tired of doing this. That's good information to have.)

Entrepreneurs run in cycles; balance isn't appealing.

Let yourself run in cycles. Enjoy the ride.

As entrepreneurs, we need backend, delivery/completion people.

Entrepreneurs are idea people. We start stuff. We don't always finish stuff, or dot the 'i's and/or cross the 't's. We need detail/delivery people but they don't usually work well with this type of person.

Entrepreneurs do get carried way. Entrepreneurs WANT to surround themselves with people who have an opinion, even if we ignore it. (In many cases, someone will say something important and the entrepreneur will ignore/ dismiss it, and then two weeks later they're doing exactly what was suggested. Happens all the time. That's just how we work. Knowledge is power.)

There. Doesn't that feel better? The next time you have a conversation with yourself about something in your business, remember your own needs - the ones that are natural to how you run as an entrepreneur.

This chapter was adapted from the How to Coach
Anyone collection produced by Andrea J. Lee under
exclusive global license from CoachVille.

"Learning is what happens when you don't know what to do. To learn more, let yourself not know, be uncertain, and unsure. Then, watch."

ANDREA LEE

CHAPTER 15

Asking Better Questions

As we near the end of this book, there's an important topic that we mustn't overlook: asking better questions. In fact, if you consider your job as a businessperson includes adding value to your clients by being ahead of them, coming up with consistently perceptive, well-placed questions will be very handy.

And also make you look really smart.

What are some easy ways to advance you in this area?

Figure 2

The Advanced Question Generator

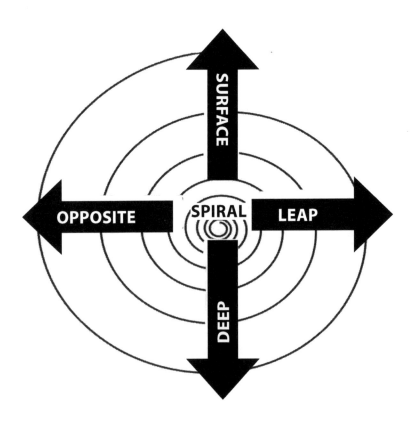

INTRODUCING THE ADVANCED QUESTION GENERATOR

The Advanced Question Generator *(see Figure 2 on page 180)* has five directions: Opposite, Surface, Deep, Leap and Spiral. Each of these is a direction you can push an ordinary question toward, to make it better, or different. You can take any ordinary question and go in any one or more directions to see what deeper question pops out.

IS THERE A USEFUL 'OPPOSITE' QUESTION?

When we're stuck and nothing we do seems to help, the question we can ask ourselves is,

> *"What if I did the opposite? What if I did the exact opposite of what I've been doing to date?"*

Applying this to question-asking, asking 'What's the opposite' leads to different questions.

Instead of getting out of bed today and asking the same question you've asked for months or years,

> *"How do I make more money today doing what I do in my business?"*

The Advanced Question Generator invites you to consider,

> *"What could I do that's the opposite of what I was planning on doing today?"*

'How do I make less money in my business?' may seem like a useless question at first, but experience has shown that the answers can lead to breakthrough insights that solve the original problem.

Just don't get mired in determine the 'exact' opposite question. Use the principle of 'opposite.'

Those of you familiar with the character George Costanza from the Seinfeld show will need no help with this!

IS THERE A USEFUL 'SURFACE' QUESTION?

What is a more surface, simpler question than the question you're asking? What is maybe even a shallower question that you could ask?

Original question: *"How do I make more money today doing what I do in my business?"*

Possible 'Surface' question: *"How do I make more money today?"*

Rationale: Letting go of one of the constraints – making money in the business, opens up the potential answers, making it easier. Perhaps making some money, any money, regardless of where it comes from, is a helpful question on this day.

Original question: *"I'm exhausted and I have a ton of travel coming up that I have to go to, and I can't cancel but I'm exhausted. What should I do?"*

Possible 'Surface' question: *"How do I stop travelling so much on business?"*

Possible 'Surface' question: *"How do I stop being so exhausted?"*

Rationale: Breaking down complex situations into their component parts, and asking separate questions about each can shed some different light. Suddenly it seems more solve-able! After answering the 'Surface' questions and returning to the original question, we can see real progress.

IS THERE A USEFUL 'DEEPER' QUESTION?

What's the deeper question that you could ask? Relative to your original question, what goes deeper, what's more complex? Can we reveal more subtleties and context?

Original question: *"How do I make more money today doing what I do in my business?"*

Possible 'Deeper' question: *"How do I make $10,000 more money each month, doing what I do in my business right now or, adding some new services, or adding to the members of the team?"*

Rationale: Being clearer, in this case by specifying $10,000 per month, forces the brain to sharpen its focus and come up with answers that are more concrete. A vague question becomes more know-able. Different potential answers show up. Adding possibilities creates complexity and reveals options. Rather than keeping ourselves to solutions involving one person, asking the 'Deeper' question, we can brainstorm outside that box.

IS THERE A USEFUL 'LEAP' OF A QUESTION?

What's a question that contextualizes the future? How can you take the timeframe of your initial question and zoom out? Try to take into account a wider swatch of time by 'Leaping' the question.

Original question: *"What should we say to the person who wants a refund?"*

Possible 'Leap' question: *"What should we say to the person who wants a refund, and all future people who may ask for refunds?"*

Rationale: Answering the original question may very well be good enough in some situations. However the 'Leap question is a cut above: proactive and thorough. It invites us to over-deliver and create an evergreen solution to something that may recur in the business. It solves the problem down to its roots.

CAN I 'SPIRAL' THE QUESTION?

Lastly, the spiral in the middle of the Advanced Question Generator represents drilling deeper with your original question. Look for the second, third, fourth, fifth question in the same spot.

Original question: *"How can we increase our profitability?"*

Possible 'Spiral' questions:

"How can we increase our income?"

"How can we decrease our expenses?"

"Can we pay off our debt faster?"

"Can we downsize our team and get the same amount of work done?"

"Should we review our tax planning strategy?"

"Have we checked our prices lately, are we competitive?"

Rationale: Asking the same question repeatedly is a little like playing one note on the tuba and hoping it will turn into music. Using the shape of a spiral as inspiration, think of this as picking up the original question and turning it around. There are usually at least three other ways to ask the same question. The direction of the question matters and will reveal different things. This gets easier with practice, and can be fun to try in groups as a brainstorming exercise with fake questions.

When the time comes to debug a real problem, you'll be ready!

Businesses, and the humans in them, are complex, and the daily challenges we face are infinite. Acquiring the ability to ask better questions is the mark of a forward-thinking business person. In these times of rapid change, where we can get a million answers from Wikipedia.org and Google.com, the ability to ask the perfect question? Is a non-negotiable must.

A FINAL NOTE...

There's no need to try all five directions in the Advanced Question Generator every time. With experience, you'll develop an intuition for the kinds of questions your clients (and you!) respond best to.

Conclusion

Speaking one's truth, firmly and fairly, in a way that can be heard, and simultaneously remain open to the other side, is, from my vantage point, the definitive skill of our times. A leader, entrepreneur, activist – any citizen, really – and their capacity to navigate change, and shape outcomes, can be measured by this skill.

This book has attempted to give depth and body to exactly how the major difficult conversations businesses run into can be handled and how we can grow into the leadership that's so sorely needed in all arenas.

As someone who was not encouraged to have her own opinions to begin with, much less to express them…

And as someone who supports leaders on their journey from fearful or timid to bold and influential…

I have great belief in the potential within us, and I commit to continuing this conversation in every way that helps. Businesses like ours can be vehicles for peace, or, sources of conflicts. My wish is for the battlefield of communication called entrepreneurship to find a path to peace.

Next time a tough conversation is needed, and you hear the words 'We Need to Talk,' I hope that instead of feeling fearful or anxious, you'll have access to a sense of calm, and a deep well of strength and capability.

WHERE ARE YOU NOW?

As you finish reading this book, I have a last request: that you take a few minutes to reassess yourself using the following questions from page 18?

The Inner and Outer Conflict Assessment for People in Business

When I think of my clients, I have positive feelings about working with them.

UNTRUE									TRUE
1	2	3	4	5	6	7	8	9	10

I am confident that my plans for growth will bear fruit.
UNTRUE   TRUE
1   2   3   4   5   6   7   8   9   10

When I think of my team, including contractors, employees, vendors or suppliers, I have positive feelings about their contributions.
UNTRUE   TRUE
1   2   3   4   5   6   7   8   9   10

My family and friends do not tell me they're concerned about how much I work.
UNTRUE   TRUE
1   2   3   4   5   6   7   8   9   10

I have fear about meeting my financial obligations.
UNTRUE   TRUE
1   2   3   4   5   6   7   8   9   10

When I have a challenging situation to handle, I can calmly do what's needed.
UNTRUE   TRUE
1   2   3   4   5   6   7   8   9   10

I feel equipped to start and hold challenging business conversations of all kinds.
UNTRUE   TRUE
1   2   3   4   5   6   7   8   9   10

Our Mission

Below is the mission of the work we do at 'We Need to Talk.' Be sure to visit www.weneedtotalkguide.com if you're interested in follow-up teaching classes for the major themes of the book. We hope you'll seize the momentum and turn ideas and inspiration into integration and implementation, today.

We are here to shape the conversation in the world.

We are here to help you do the same.

We are here to hold space for the impossible dreams to become possible.

We are here to create peace in the world through the entrepreneurial spirit.

We are here to experience, model, stimulate and uplift others and make ideas real.

Want More?

To go deeper, from inspiration to implementation and integration of the concepts in this book and more, be sure to visit Wealthy Thought Leader University at www.WealthyThoughtLeader.com.

If you bought this book as part of our book birthday celebrations, you're likely eligible for additional gifts, including in-person workshops. And, if you're interested in licensing the 'We Need to Talk' concepts, you'll want to be in touch. Write us at support@wealthythoughtleader.com with your questions.

You can also get an online copy of the Inner and Outer Conflict Assessment for Business People, and a complimentary exploratory session with one of our team, at

www.WealthyThoughtLeader.com/conflictassessment

About the Author

ANDREA LEE is founder + CEO of Thought Partners International, which does business online under the identity **'Wealthy Thought Leader'** — an internationally-known boutique coaching and training company that has helped thousands of entrepreneurs prove their original business concepts, design offerings that break new ground, and sell in lucrative ways that feel good.

She is also Director of Strategic Planning for the **Indrani's Light Foundation**, a global non-profit committed to eradicating domestic violence.

Andrea is also the previous author of **Multiple Streams of Coaching Income** and **Pink Spoon Marketing**, and was named by Seth Godin and Fast Company Magazine as a Bull Market company helping clients stand out and be remarkable.

In addition to her 18+ years as a business mentor, Andrea is a domestic violence survivor, recovered abuse perpetrator and a believer that all things, both good and bad, can and must be learned from. She considers herself an activist-entrepreneur.

To find out more about Andrea, visit:
www.AndreaJLee.com
www.WealthyThoughtLeader.com

Made in the USA
San Bernardino, CA
13 June 2015